Decorations to Dazzle

by Sue Schofield

Publisher *Viking Loom Ltd.,*
22 High Petergate,
York. YO1 7EH
First published in Great Britain in 2004 by the Viking Loom Ltd.

Photography *Graham Schofield*

Design and Print *The Max Design & Print co.*

ISBN *0-9547794-0-1*

Acknowledgements

I would like to say thank you to my husband Steve for his help and support; to Romy Cordingley for her encouragement; to my son Graham for the splendid photography and to Lyn Hirons who inspired me to look again at the possibilities of polystyrene.

Introduction

I have always loved the Christmas season and as a child had no difficulty in believing that Father Christmas did indeed come down the large chimney of our 16th century farmhouse. In the northern hemisphere with cold days and long dark winter nights we need the cheerfulness of glitter and gold, rich reds and evergreens. I have spent many Christmases in the tropics where bright sunlight creates less need for colourful decoration. Yet even when living in a desert region I found myself painting a thorn bush white and hanging baubles on it for the delight of my young son. Change the colours to silver and pink or purple and you have a celebratory summery look ideal for decorating a marquee, or continue the colour scheme of your soft furnishings. The choice is yours.

The decorations are not difficult and many require no sewing at all. Some need a line of backstitch. They can be completed in an evening, are very satisfying to do and make wonderful gifts. They can become addictive! I like the idea of making a new decoration each year for one's children, grandchildren, relatives, friends or oneself! If at all possible put the date on. Children also get a great deal of satisfaction from creating these baubles. I find it best to draw the lines and do the cutting for them so that there is no chance of an accident. You might also want to put the loop in place. The boys often choose the colours of their favourite football team! Please remember that decorations are not toys and should be kept away from young children. Have fun making them!

Sue Schofield
Yorkshire, 2004

Contents

Materials for making baubles

Polystyrene Balls

Polystyrene, which is now made in a wide variety of different shapes, has been available in the UK for the past twelve years and for longer still on the Continent. Here we are using a selection of balls. The manufacturers number the sizes by using the diameter, so that for example a No 10 ball is actually a ball 10cm in diameter. To check the diameter stand the ball on a firm surface and hold a ruler, with markings which go to the bottom of the ruler, next to it. Place another ruler or book across the top of the ball and read the measurement (ball Fig.01). In theory to find the circumference you need to multiply the diameter by pi, which is 3.1416. Alternatively pin a piece of thin 3mm ribbon around the circumference and measure it against a ruler.

You need to know the size to estimate the amount of trim you need and an exact circumference is necessary in some patterns. I find the most useful sized balls are Nos. 7, 10 and 12, i.e. measured by their diameter 7cm, 10cm and 12cm. Anything smaller than 7cm is really too small to work with. The 7cm ball, which is a bit smaller than a tennis ball, is the ideal size for hanging on a standard Christmas tree or on bare branches. The 8cm size, a little larger, is useful if you want to put cross stitch or stumpwork on to a ball. It is not a size I personally use very often. The 10cm ball, which is grapefruit sized, and the 12cm ball which is larger, more like a melon, are much bigger. I hang these in doorways, in front of windows, from the ceiling, in the corners of rooms and they look fantastic. The next size ball is a 15cm which comes in two parts and is hollow. This is more like a small soccer ball. It is more difficult to work, being hollow. I have given instructions and quantities for 7, 10 and 12cm balls as these have proved to be the most popular sizes. The chart below provides a handy reference.

Size (diameter)	Description	Circumference	
7cm ball	Tennis ball	22cm	8 5/8"
8cm ball		25cm	10"
10cm ball	Grapefruit	31.5cm	12 1/2"
12cm ball	Melon	37.7cm	14 3/4"
15cm hollow ball in 2 parts	Football	47cm	18 1/2"

Fabrics

You can use a wide range of fabrics to cover these baubles and you will achieve different effects. Many years ago I tried using cotton fabrics. I was disappointed with the result and found the cottons difficult to use. The softer, more malleable fabrics work better; silk is easier than cotton in this respect. There is a wealth of exotic, glittery, shiny and sequined fabric available now which can be contrasted with sumptuous tactile velvets, brocades or other textured fabrics. You just have to try and if you are not pleased with your initial choice, try another fabric. Keep a look out for suitable fabrics, not only in fabric shops but in markets and Asian stores. Most of these fabrics are inexpensive and look fantastic. I can still occasionally be tempted by an expensive hologrammed stretch fabric (used to make leotards and dance costumes). These stretch fabrics contain spandex which makes them particularly useful for creating swirling designs but they are more expensive. I love velvets too.

Fabrics to avoid are the ones that fray. They are not impossible to use but make life so difficult that I don't bother with them. I also avoid the shiny cheap 'paper lamé' fabrics because not only do they fray but the fabric is so thin it is easily damaged while making the bauble. Many of these fabrics crush or crease easily and should not be folded. They are also difficult to iron. Several times I have returned home with a 'fat quarter' of fabric and found that where the right sides have been touching for some time the fabric is damaged. I buy small quantities of fabric, cut them into squares and store them flat, usually under the spare room bed. Clean pizza boxes are also useful for keeping fabrics flat until you need them. Velvets are best hung.

These baubles do not use large quantities of fabric. Try and buy the smallest amount possible - a quarter of a metre or yard rather than half a metre or yard. If you have to buy a larger quantity then try swapping some with a friend. Christmas colours do not change much. Red and gold remain the favourites and any left-over fabrics can be put aside for other future Christmas projects. My collection of fabrics has been built up over many years. I add to it frequently.

There are some good bargains to be had after Christmas and I enjoy enriching the colourless days of a northern January and February by creating more decorations. By the time Easter arrives my family politely ask if they can be taken down!

Velvets

There is a good selection of suitable velvet available. Do not be tempted to buy a piece of velvet furnishing fabric however as it will be too thick. You need the dress weight. Velvet was originally made from silk but it is now made from a variety of fibres; viscose, acetate, rayon, silk and cotton for example. Cotton is the most difficult to use. You can also find embroidered velvet, at a price! A mixture of viscose and acetate will give a two-tone effect. Sometimes the velvet has an added texture applied, called embossing, which reflects the light in different ways. Some velvets are stretchy and some 'give' but do not stretch.

My favourites are good quality crushed velvets – no need to worry about them becoming creased! A visit to Britain's only mill still producing dress weight velvet taught me that there are three sorts of crushed velvet. First there is the 'hand crushed' (by the mill) which looks rather like the bark of a tree. Then comes 'supercrush', which is similar but crushed by machine. An 'antique' finish is achieved by putting the fabric through a rinsing process and then tumble drying it. This produces an all-over mottled effect. All can be made into wonderfully rich glowing decorations. There are also various velours which are suitable.

Sequined fabrics

What I think of as sequined fabrics are foil-printed in various shapes on to a polyester base. These are very useful, come in a range of colours and are pliable. So far I have discovered ones with small, 3mm round sequins which are ideal for use on the 7cm ball or in complicated patterns. Next comes a round sequin which is bigger so of more use on the 10 or 12cm ball. Then there are fabrics with diamonds – good on the 12cm ball. Just remember when using diamonds that you must cut out all the pieces the same way or the diamonds on the ball will not go the same way.

Microdot Foil

Another useful stretchy fabric, 100% polyester. If you look closely you will see that these shiny fabrics are made up of tiny dots on either a black or white background. They are easy to use and do not fray. You can also get foil printed velour.

Stretch Foil

Made of a mixture of nylon, polyester and spandex in an array of brilliant colours these are wonderful and stretchy, but more expensive. You can also get a fabric with small dots of colour on spandex, with a variety of different printing effects and there is hologram on spandex.

Mirror Lamé

These fabrics are brilliantly shiny and make me think of liquid metals. They are not expensive. Use them carefully as the edges of the fabric can split. Allow a bit extra when you cut out the shapes.

Trims

A variety of trims can be used. I prefer beaded ones as they reflect the light well. They consist of pearls which are fused or moulded on to a string. They come in a range of pastel colours as well as gold and silver. You may even find red, purple or green. They are made in several sizes – 2.5mm, 3mm and 4mm. I find the 2.5mm rather too small but find the 3mm the most useful for the 7cm ball. A facetted trim in 4mm size is also available in gold and silver and adds even more sparkle to the decoration. I use this on the 10cm and 12cm balls whenever possible. On the more complicated balls the larger beading is often not appropriate. You do not have to use a beaded trim. In Design No. 4 I used two different flat braids, rather than a beaded trim and in Design. 8 the diamond ball, I used a flat braid also.

Findings

This is the name given to a range of small items used in jewellery making which are inexpensive but often difficult to find. They are very useful and I always buy them when I see them and I am always on the look out for new ones. The one I use most is a filigree bell cap which comes in several sizes. It has a hole at the top through which I push the ribbon hanging loop. You can also use it at the bottom of the bauble. It is not essential to use findings but they finish the bauble and also cover the area where the beaded trim crosses over. You may well find something better. I also use a wire spiral cut in half. This is useful when attaching a tassel with a thick loop which will not go through a bell cap finding. A long thin cone has been used in Designs 14 and 15.

Embellishments

I feel that a bauble does not look finished unless there is something at the bottom. On 7cm balls a 12mm gold bead attached with a corsage pin looks good. As it is difficult to find large gold balls I use tassels, bells or crystal drops. You can of course make your own tassels but gold and silver tassels are readily available. You can also use a beaded tassel.

Pins and needles

You will need a packet of Bead and Sequin pins in either nickel or gilt, depending on whether you are working with silver or gold. These are short pins which are ideal for anchoring the trim.

Corsage pins (a 4.5cm [1½"] pin with an egg-shaped bead at the top) are usually available in pearl, gold and more rarely silver. These are useful at the bottom of a ball and can also be used at the top. Hat pins are well worth looking out for, or you can make your own. I usually attach the top finding with a plain pin with a head big enough to keep the finding safely in place.

A large needle is needed to pierce the balls and thread the ribbon through. A 17.5cm (7") needle is fine for small balls but a 20cm (10") mattress needle will work on all sizes.

Ribbon

I use 3mm gold or silver lamé ribbon to make a hanging loop but any coloured ribbon would be suitable as would cord. Designs 15 and 16 use a 25mm (1") wide ribbon as well.

Other items

You will need three different cutting tools; a craft knife or scalpel with a thin blade, scissors for cutting fabric and a smaller pair of scissors with long thin blades for trimming back the fabric.

For pushing the fabric into the cracks you need something that is not too thick or too pointed. I use an embossing tool. This has blunt rounded points at both ends, one larger than the other. I can push the fabric in without piercing it. You can use the corner of a plastic credit or loyalty card. This works well for many people for the simple designs. Some people use the tip of a thin metal nail file.

A self-erasing pen can be useful for marking guide lines (as in the swirling ball).

You will also need a tape measure or ruler and a couple of biros (ball-point pens) in different colours.

General instructions for Bauble making

Many balls come with markings on them and all should have a manufacturer's line around them which I shall call the circumference. Start by checking out your ball; see how many segments, if any, it is divided into and what size it is. (See the chart under Polystyrene Balls on page 4). If your ball is not marked into segments you will need to do so following the specific instructions given with each of the individual designs.

1. Put a biro dot at the top and bottom of the ball first.

2. I find the easiest way to divide the ball into segments is to use a piece of thin 3mm ribbon as a measure and different instructions are given for doing this depending on how many segments are required for the particular design. The ribbon is more pliable than a tape measure. Draw alongside the ribbon lightly with a biro. If you make a mistake either paint over the wrong line with typewriter correcting fluid like Tipp-Ex or go over all the correct lines with a different coloured pen. A disappearing or self-erasing pen is useful.

3. To cut the lines you have marked (following the instructions given with each of the different designs) use a sharp thin blade. Work slowly and carefully so that pieces of polystyrene do not break away. You need to cut into the polystyrene fairly deeply,

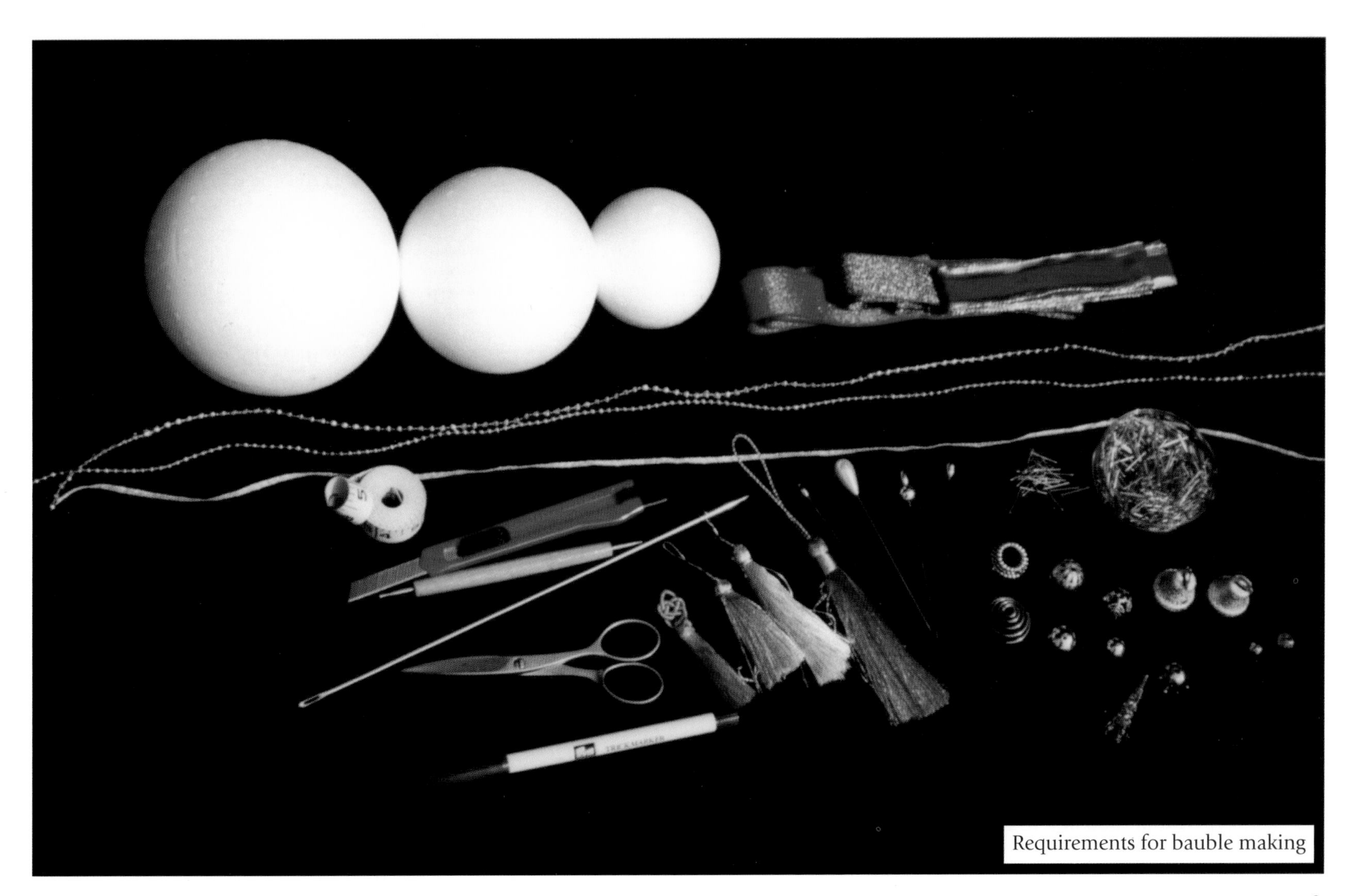

Requirements for bauble making

1.5cm or 1/4", but remember you are not segmenting an orange! This is particularly important if you are working on the large hollow ball.

4. I like to make a hole all the way through the ball for the hanging loop. This is more secure than just pinning a loop on the top. Stand the ball on its bottom and drive a long needle straight through. You may need to do this in stages if it is a big ball. Sometimes it helps to heat the needle. If your needle does not come out exactly where you want it to, try again. You do not have to be too exact as it will not show. Sometimes you can ease the needle over. If you do not have a long needle you could use a knitting needle or skewer to make the hole.

5. To make the hanging loop, fold the ribbon in half and thread the folded end through the eye of the needle. Push the needle and ribbon through the ball. Remove the needle and if you are not attaching a tassel, knot the two loose ends with a double knot so that it will not disappear up inside the ball. Trim the ends and the knot should lie flush against the bottom of the ball where it will be covered by the trimming later.

6. If you want to add a tassel thread the loop of the tassel through a suitable finding (bell cap for a tassel with a fine loop or a half spiral or collar type finding for a tassel with a thicker one) then on to the ribbon and tie a single knot, as the loop of the tassel is going to be drawn up into the ball. You may find that you have left too large a hanging loop at the top of the ball and need to tie another knot at the base of the ball so that the hanging loop is the desired length. Trim off the ends of the ribbon below the knot and pull on the ribbon hanging loop gently so that the knot disappears inside the ball, pulling the loop of the tassel up with it. Do not pull it up tight at this stage as you need room to work. (See Design 1 *Fig.3* page 15).

7. If you wish to design your own balls and make templates for cutting out fabric you will need some thin paper. When you have marked and cut the ball, pin your piece of paper over the section and trace around the outlines. You need thin paper to be able to mould it to the contours of the ball. You can then use this pattern to make a more solid template.

8. When cutting out fabric, lay your template on the fabric, right side up, and cut out roughly 1cm (3/8") beyond the template all around (this extra fabric is pushed into the ball). Do not mark the fabrics with pen or chalk as it will show and is not necessary. Do this for all fabric templates given in this book.

9. Before you start putting the fabric in place pin the hanging loop securely down against the ball so that it does not get cut off by mistake. If it does you have the choice of either replacing it with a new piece of ribbon or removing what remains and making a new loop and pinning it securely to the top of the ball.

10. You only need small quantities of fabric to make one of these designs. A quarter of a metre (yard) will be more than sufficient

and will leave plenty to create several baubles. Audition your fabrics. Lay them against the ball and ask yourself whether: a) they are suitable for the size of ball. Ensure that the pattern is not too large. b)Does the fabric need to be particularly soft and malleable for a more complicated design or one with curves. c)Do the chosen colours make a good contrast or complement each other. Are they suitable? (e.g. green fabric intended for a green Christmas tree will not show up, although turquoise will). d)Would a contrast of textures be good? e.g. a smooth velvet with a sequined fabric; a textured crushed velvet with a smooth mirror lamé or microdot foil. Often it is a question of trial and error. Sometimes, looking at a finished ball, I decide that, no, one of the fabrics does not look good, so I take it out and replace it. I have been amazed at just how good some children's rather weird, in my view, colour combinations have worked out. Experiment!

The fabric is going to be pushed down into the crack created by the knife. All the ends will get pushed in so you have a nice smooth finish with no rough edges. If the odd fabric is not staying in place as you would wish, push a small pin down into the crack to stabilise it. These joints will then be covered by a line of beaded trim or other braid.

11. The beaded trims are best attached using small sequin and bead pins – normal pins are too long to use. As it is extremely difficult to pierce the beading I cross two pins over each other, trapping the beading. On sharp curves and at points of diamonds extra pins are required. As a general guide start by laying the beaded trim over a join at the top of the ball and pin about 0.5cm (1/4") down and then pin again 0.5cm or 1/4" from the bottom. I avoid pinning in the middle as you can see the indentation. You can use the beaded trim as one long continuous length. To avoid creating a mountain of beading at the top and bottom instead of going straight across the ball you can go down the next segment. This will be covered up by a finding later. In every design I have calculated the amount of beaded trim needed as this is the most variable component.

11. All the designs in this book use a finding at the top of the ball through which the hanging loop passes. At the base of the ball you can use a hanging decoration or a corsage or hat pin plus a large bead.

12. I recommend that you read the full instructions given for creating Design 1 before creating any other design.

Design No.1 – Basic Ball

Design Nos. 2, 3 and 4

DESIGN NO. 1
BASIC BALL
Eight segments

Refer to the colour photograph page 12

This ball can be made in any size from a wide range of fabrics. I like to contrast textures. For the 7cm ball I chose crushed velvet and a small sequin dot. For a 10cm ball I used a shiny fabric with a hologrammed pattern on it which I thought would be shown to advantage. For a 12cm ball I used a diamond shaped sequin fabric and some wonderful red velvet with an embossed pattern on it. On the two bigger balls I have used 4mm faceted trim to give added sparkle. On the 7cm ball I used a 3mm beaded trim.

1. Start by marking the top and bottom of the ball with a biro dot. You will notice the manufacturer's line running around the middle, which I will call the circumference.

2. If your ball has not been marked off into eight segments (by the manufacturer), attach the end of a piece of 3mm ribbon at the top with a pin. Wrap the ribbon around the ball, temporarily pinning it again at the bottom. The ball is now divided into two. Run a biro lightly alongside the ribbon. Move the ribbon around the ball, dividing it into quarters and then eighths (*Fig.1*). Mathematical precision is not required. If your ball is already marked, go over the marks with biro so that you will be able to see where to cut.

3. Cut fairly deeply – 1.5cm or 1/2" – into your biro marked lines with a long narrow blade.

4. Stand the ball on its bottom and drive the needle straight through. With luck this should come out exactly where you want it to. If not, do it again. Sometimes you can pull the needle to one side. For the bigger balls you may need to push the needle through in stages. It is not important to be too exact.

5. Fold the piece of ribbon in half and thread the folded part through the eye of the needle. Pull the needle and ribbon

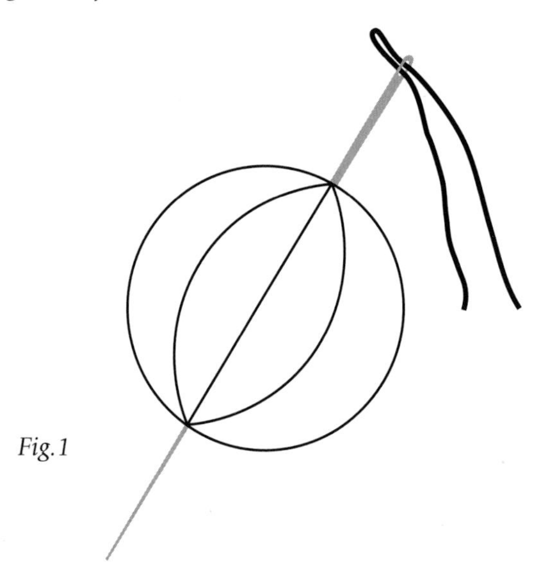

Fig.1

through the ball (*Fig.1*). Remove the needle; knot the ends of the ribbon twice, unless you wish to add a hanging decoration in which case it is added *before the ribbon is knotted*, see the next step. Check to see the loop at the top of the ball is the length you want. If it is too long make another knot. Then trim the ribbon ends and pull upon the loop until the knot is lying against the ball. The knot should be big enough not to disappear up into the ball (*Fig.2*).

6. If you want to add a hanging decoration such as a bell, tassel, crystal etc, this needs to be threaded on to the ribbon *before* it is knotted. I find it useful where possible, to put something between the decoration (bell, tassel crystal etc) and the ball. This covers up where the beaded trim crosses over. *Fig.3* shows a bell cap finding. Push one end of the ribbon through the centre hole of the finding. Thread the tassel on to the ribbon and push the ribbon back up through the finding. Knot the ends of the ribbon once and trim. The knot should be a single one as this can then be pulled up so that it disappears inside the ball. The decoration ensures that the ribbon hanging loop is not able to be pulled right through the ball. Draw up the ribbon hanging loop at the top of the ball gently so that the knot is now invisible inside the ball. Do not pull it up too close to the bottom of the ball as you will need room to work. *Fig.4* shows a half spiral finding.

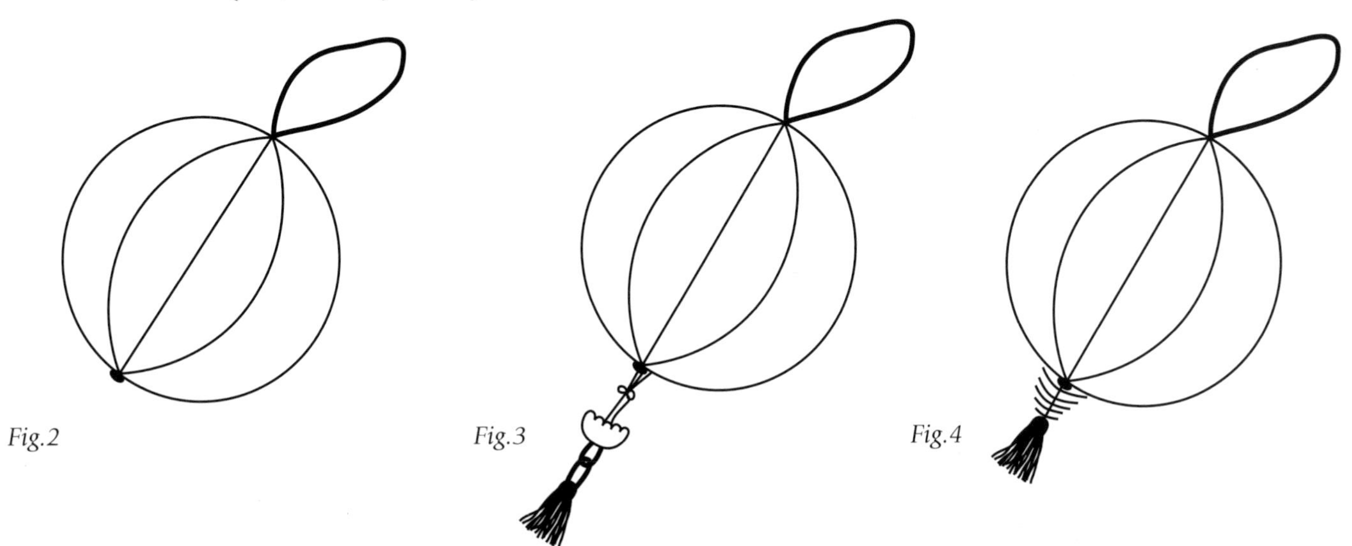

Fig.2 *Fig.3* *Fig.4*

7. Trace Template A in your chosen size on to a piece of card or paper. Lay this template on to your fabric and cut out around it roughly, adding a 1cm (3/8") seam allowance (*Fig.5*). Do not mark the fabric with a pencil, pen or chalk.

8. It is best to start with the "easiest fabric" which is the thinnest fabric. Velvets, being heavier, are best left until last. Pin the ribbon loop out of the way while you are working so that it does not get cut off by mistake. Lay a piece of fabric over one of the segments. Starting at the widest point, the middle, and using an embossing tool, a thin nail file tip or the corner of a plastic credit card, push the fabric gently into the crack (*Fig.6*). Do this all round the segment. Check that the fabric has not come away and then cut off the excess fabric. Push all the fabric edges well down into the cracks so that the fabric lies smoothly. Leave the next segment blank and continue using the same fabric to do segments 3, 5 and 7.

9. Proceed with the second fabric in exactly the same way. I sometimes stop after putting the first of the second fabrics in place and check that I really do like the two fabrics together. If you are happy with your fabric selection complete the segments using the second fabric.

10. Take the beading and pin it securely at the top. Use small sequin and bead pins for this. Lay the beading over the joins and pin it again 0.5cm or 1/4" from the bottom. I avoid pinning in the middle as you can see the indentation when the ball is hanging up. As it is extremely difficult to pierce the beading I cross two pins over each other, trapping the beading (*Fig.7*). Continue around the segments securing the beading top and bottom. You can use the beaded trim in one long piece. To avoid creating a mountain of beading at the top and bottom instead of going straight across the ball each time, occasionally you can go down the next segment. You can also use short lengths. Whatever you do the area at the top will be covered by a finding and there will be a decoration at the bottom.

11. To finish (if you have not added a decoration at step 7), place a gold bead on to a gold headed corsage or hat pin and push it into the base of the ball. If you have attached a hanging decoration, pull up gently on the ribbon loop so that the finding fits neatly against the bottom of the ball and the decoration hangs freely.

12. To finish the top, push the narrow ribbon loop through the small hole in the top of the finding. This is easy to do using an embossing tool, tip of pencil or blunt end of a needle. If you are having difficulty, thread a sewing needle with a thread; knot the ends either side of the ribbon loop and draw the needle up through the finding. To secure the finding to the top of the ball use a plain pin with a head big enough to keep the finding in place or a corsage pin or use a few sequin pins around the base of the finding.

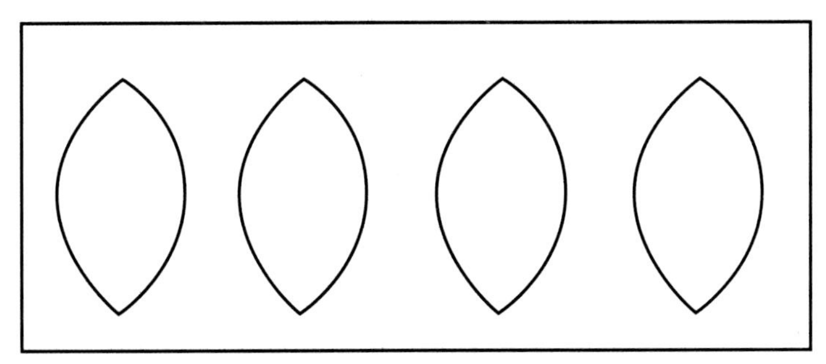

Fig.5

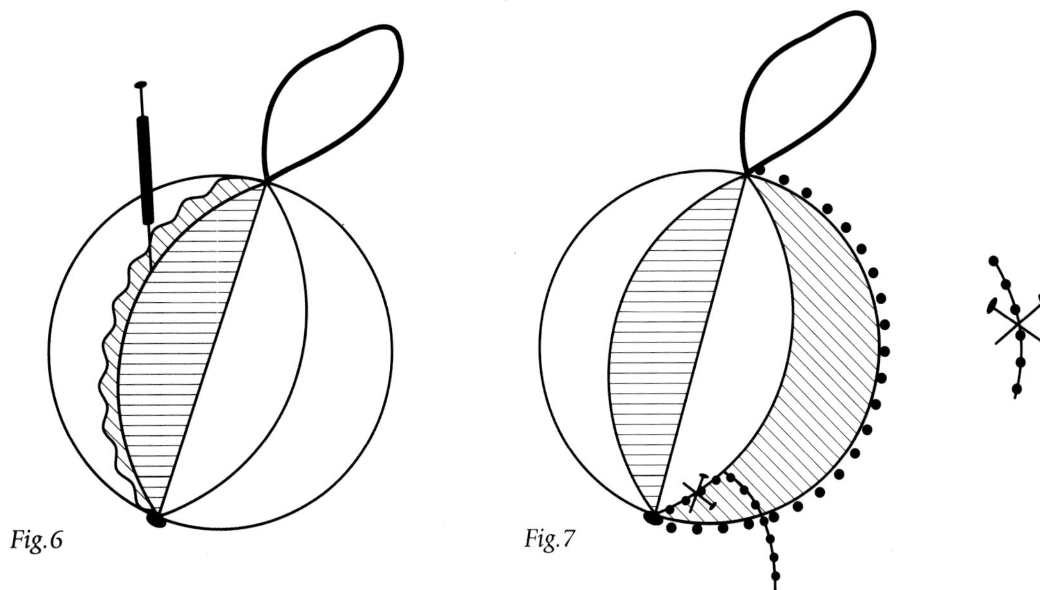

Fig.6

Fig.7

Design No. 1 – Basic Ball – Eight Segments

Ball	7cm ball	10cm ball	12cm ball
Fabric – equal amount of two different fabrics	15 x 25cm 6" x 10"	21 x 30cm 8 1/4" x 12"	24 x 34cm 9 1/2" x 13 1/2"
3mm gold ribbon	50cm (20")	60cm (2/3 yd)	1m (1yd)
Beaded trim	3mm x 1m (1yd)	4mm x 1.40m (1 2/3yd)	4mm x 1.60m (2yd)
Sequin pins	Yes	Yes	Yes
Top finding	Yes	Yes	Yes
Corsage pin + gold bead	Yes	Either	Either
Tassel, bell, crystal + finding		Or	Or

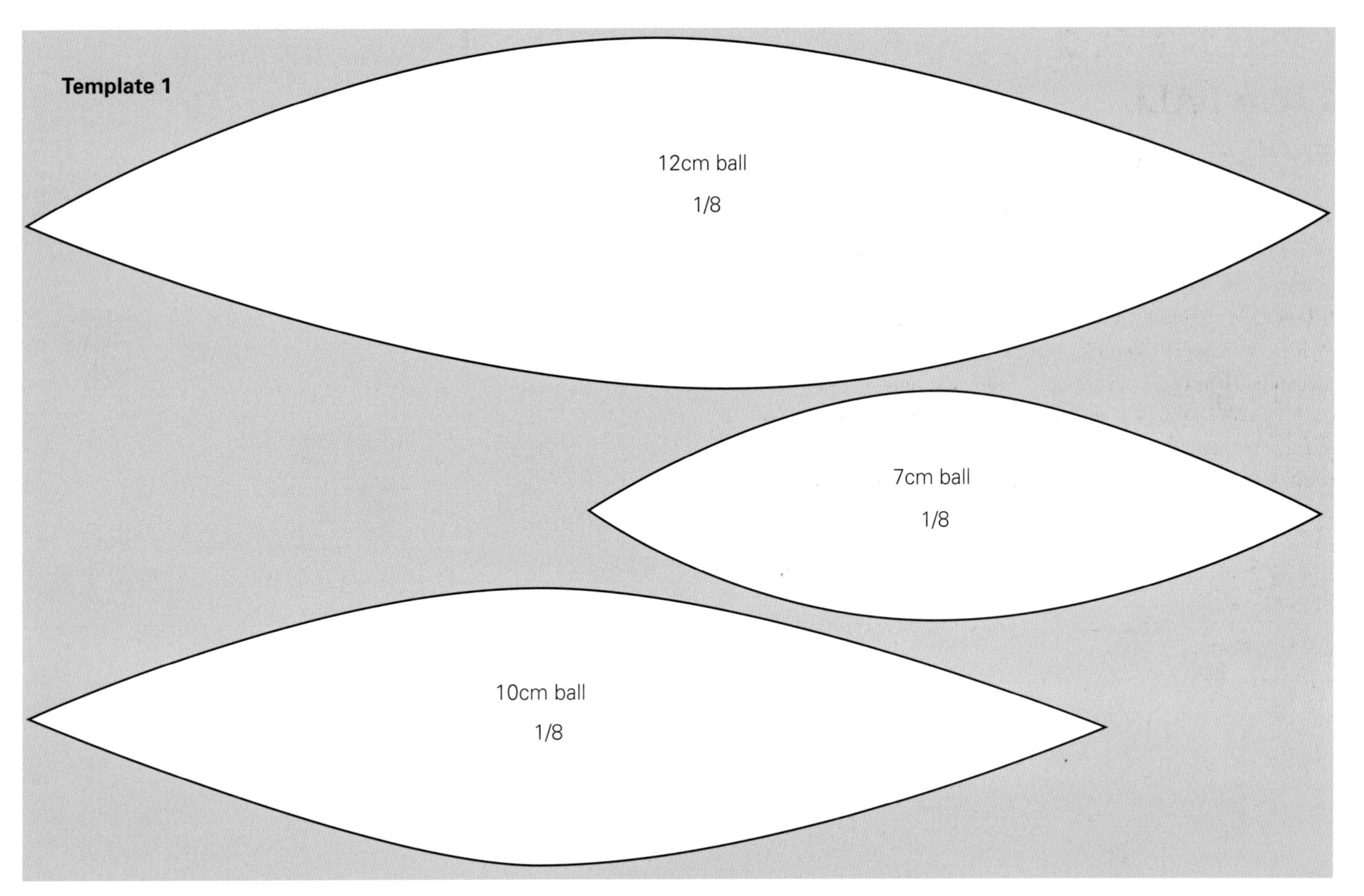
Template 1
12cm ball
1/8
7cm ball
1/8
10cm ball
1/8

DESIGN NO. 2
12cm BALL
16 Segments

Refer to the colour photograph page 13

This design takes the original eight segmented design described in Design 1 one step further. I use it on a 12cm or bigger ball. Follow steps 1–2 for Design 1. When you have divided the ball into eighths, divide each segment into half vertically so that you have sixteen segments. Continue as in Design 1 following steps 3–12 but using the template below as a fabric cutting guide. In this ball you can use more fabrics and colour combinations. Whether you alternate two colours or use many more they need to divide into 16. Some combinations are given below:

a) ABCDAECF then repeat (page 13)

b) ABAC repeat 3 times

c) ABACADAEAFAGAHAI

Design No. 2 – 16 Segmented Ball

Ball	12cm ball
Two pieces of fabric each measuring	40 x 25cm (16" x 10")
3mm gold ribbon	1m (1yd)
4mm beaded trim	3.25m (3 1/2yd)
Top finding + bottom decoration and short sequin pins	

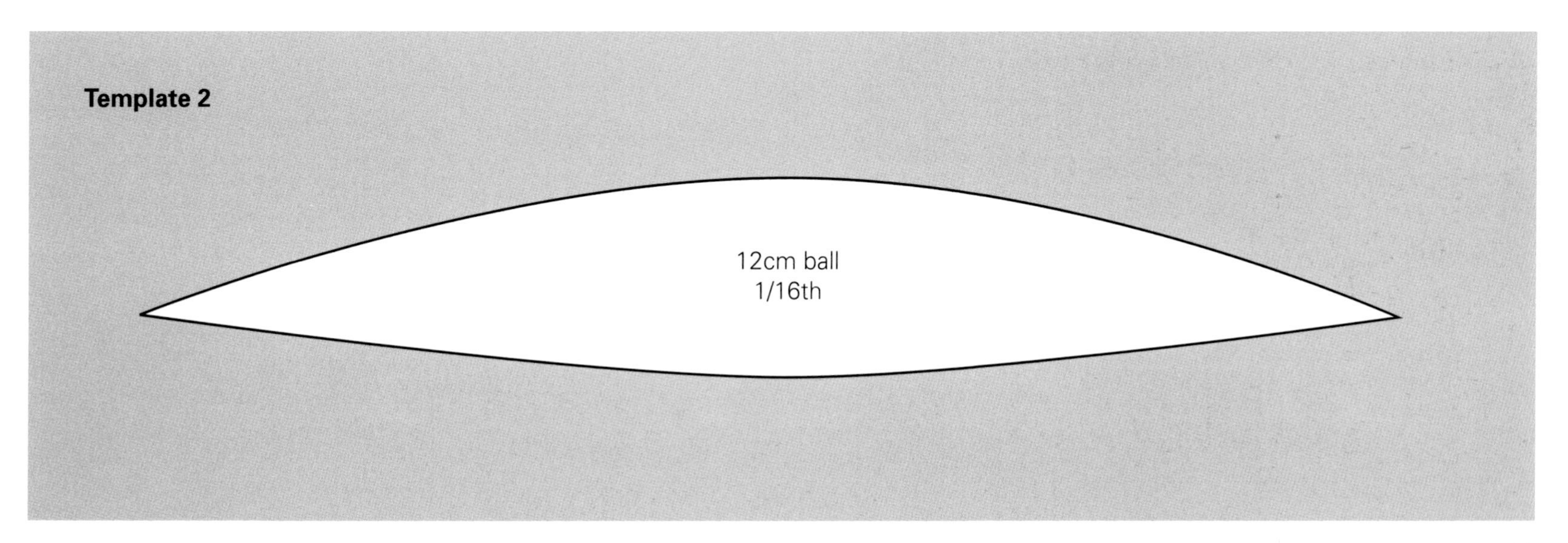

DESIGN NO. 3
10cm BALL
12 segments

Refer to the colour photograph page 13

The bauble is divided into 12 segments which creates a rich and varied look. The use of facetted beaded trim adds extra sparkle.

1. Mark the top and bottom of the ball with a biro dot.
2. Divide the ball in half with a piece of thin ribbon and make a biro line. The circumference of a 10cm ball is 31.5cm ($12^1/_2$") divided by 6 = 5.25cm. Put a pin in the end of the ribbon and put another one 5.25cm along as shown (*Fig.1*).
3. Push one pin plus ribbon into the ball where the vertical line crosses the circumference and use the second pin in the ribbon as a marker. Make a biro dot to the right of the vertical then swing the ribbon around and make a biro dot to the left (*Fig.2*). Turn the ball around and repeat the marks either side of the other vertical line. Use the ribbon to mark in the other vertical lines. You now have six vertical lines. Divide each segment again, by eye, so that you have 12 segments.
4. Continue as for Design 1, steps 3–12, pages 14, 15 and 16. Your choice of fabric needs to divide in 12. I have used three toning pinky-purple fabrics in the combination ABC repeated four times. You could equally well do ABAC repeated three times or ABCD. Experiment!!!

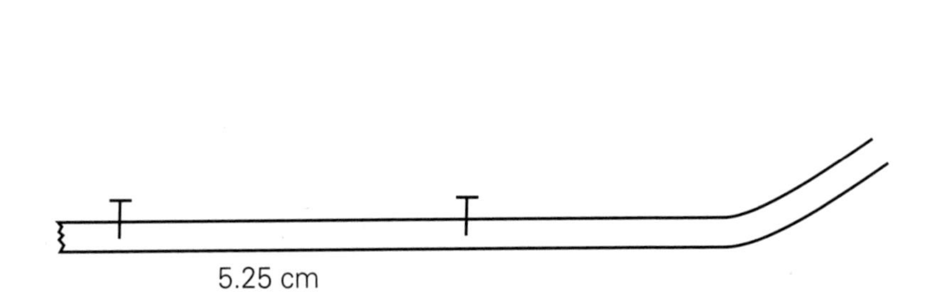

Fig.1

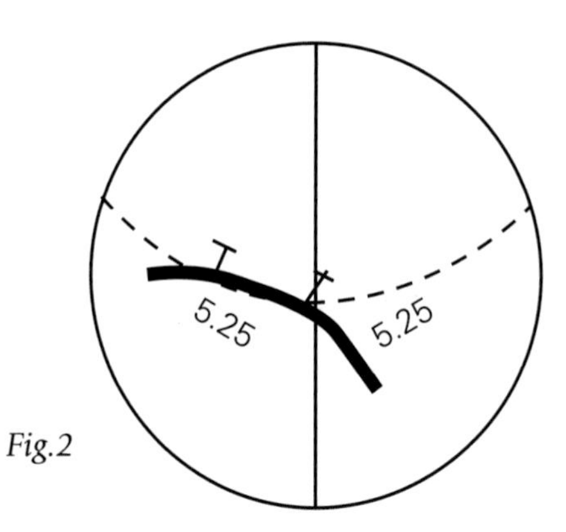

Fig.2

Design No. 3 – 12 Segmented Ball

Ball	10cm ball
Two pieces of fabric each measuring	21cm (9") square
3mm gold ribbon	60cm (2/3yd)
4mm or 3mm beaded trim	2.10m (2 1/3yd)
Top finding + bottom decoration. Short sequin pins	

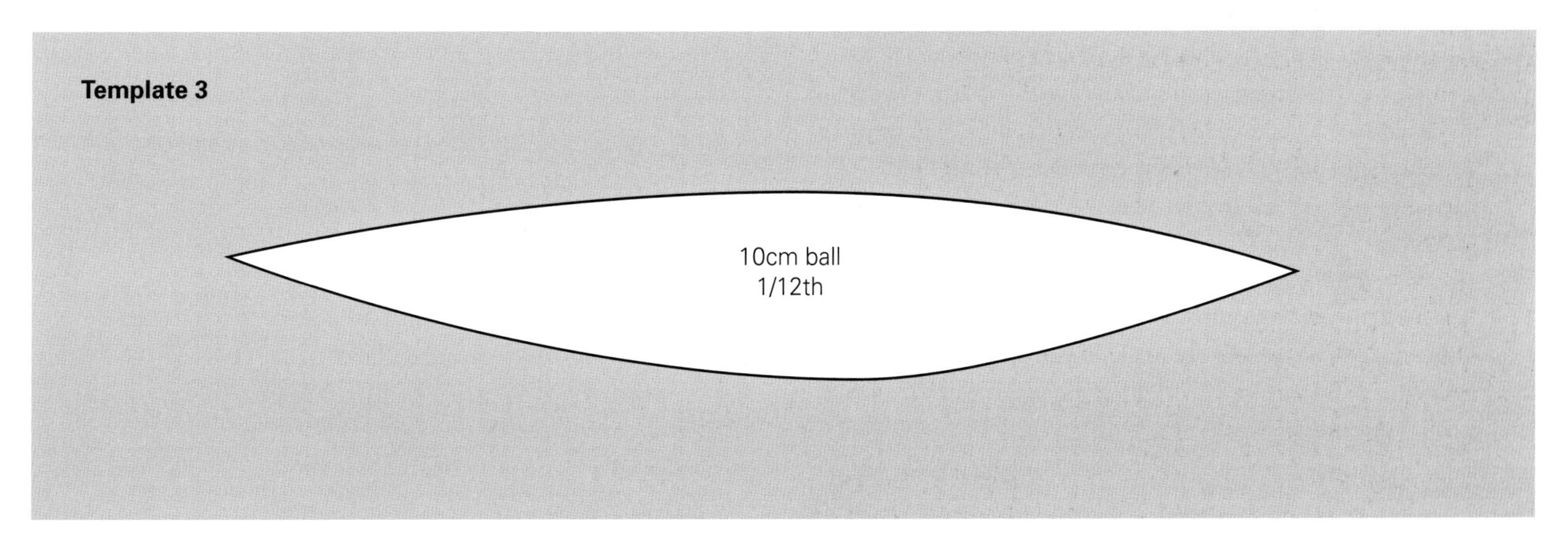

DESIGN NO. 4
LACE BRAIDED BALL

Refer to the colour photograph page 13

Occasionally I want to use a fine piece of lace or other interesting braid that I have found. As these tend to be wider than the 3mm and 4mm beaded trim that I usually use I divide a 7cm ball into sixths rather than eighths. In this instance I used plain gold fabric to cover each segment as I wanted to emphasize the braids. A 10cm or 12cm ball can also be used, divide them into eight segments as described in Design 1, step 2, page 14.

1. For a 7cm ball, begin by marking the top and bottom of the ball and divide the ball in half with a thin piece of ribbon. Draw alongside it. The circumference of a 7cm ball is 22cm ($8^5/_8$") divided by 6 = 3.66cm ($1^3/_8$"). Mark 3.66cm off along the piece of ribbon. Pin one end where the vertical line crosses the circumference and use the pin 3.66cm along as a marker and make a biro dot on the circumference. Swing the ribbon around and make another mark on the other side of the vertical line. Repeat on the second vertical line. Ink in the lines using the ribbon as a guide. It does not matter if you are not mathematically precise. The width of the braids will hide any small discrepancies.
2. Continue following Design 1, steps 3–12, pages 14, 15 and 16. Cut the polystyrene, insert the ribbon loop, knot and pin it out of the way. Put in your fabric segments but use the braid in Step 10.
3. Choosing the thinnest of your braids and pinning it near the top, place it down the middle of each segment, pinning top and bottom as you go. Then do the same with your second braid, laying it over the joins of each segment, pinning it near the top and again near the bottom.
4. Attach a bell cap finding to the top and a corsage or hat pin to the bottom. As the braids are bulkier than the beaded trim they make the finished ball look bigger than the 7cm ball of Design 1.

Design No. 4 Lace Braided Ball

Ball	7cm ball
Fabric (one piece only)	33 x 14cm (13" x 5$^{1}/_{2}$")
3mm gold ribbon	50cm (20")
Braid No. 1	75cm (30")
Braid No. 2	75cm (30")
Top finding + large headed pearl pin or hat pin. Short sequin pins	

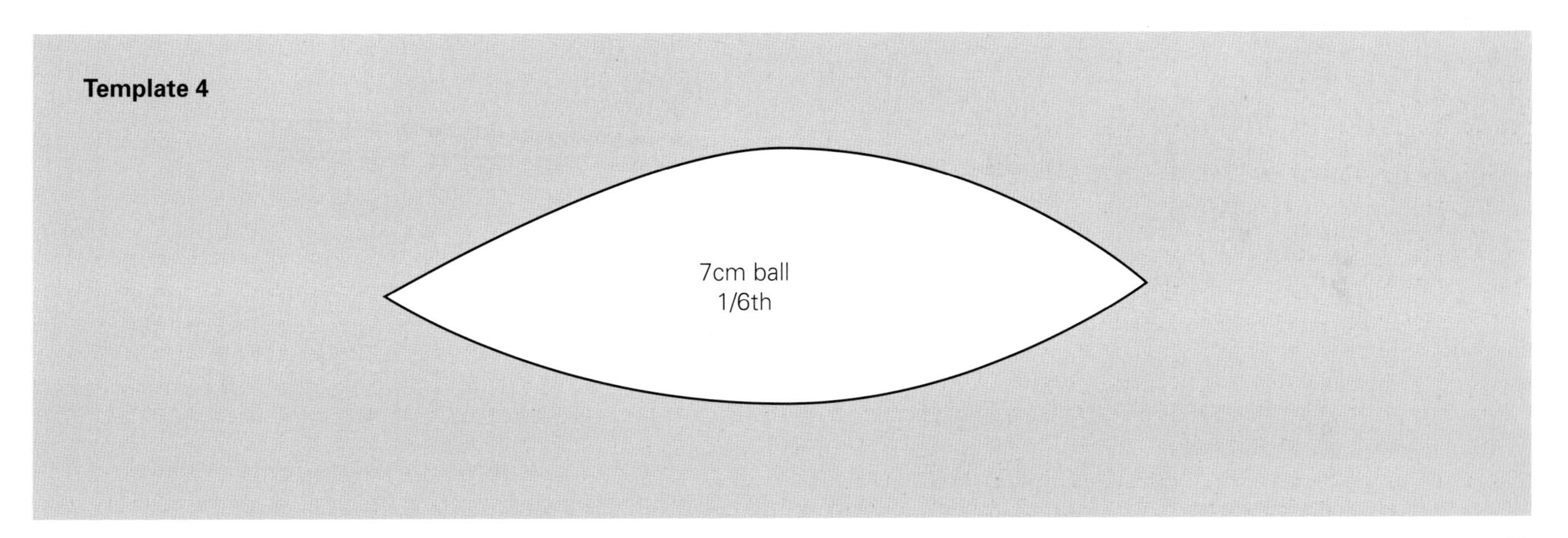

Design No. 5 – Chequered Ball

Design No. 6 – Flower Ball

DESIGN NO. 5
CHEQUERED BALL

Refer to the colour photograph page 26

The design gives a chequered effect and was inspired by the spectacular art nouveau lamps in front of the railway station at Helsinki, Finland.

1. Whichever size ball you are doing, mark the top and bottom of the ball and draw in eight segments see Design 1, step 2, page 14.

2. Using the thin ribbon place an anchor pin near one end of the ribbon and

   a) measure 5cm (2") along the ribbon for the 10cm ball and put a further pin in to mark this distance

   b) measure 6cm ($2^1/_2$") along the ribbon for the 12cm ball. (See step 3 for the 7cm ball). Push one pin and ribbon into the top of the ball and make marks where the other pin crosses the vertical lines and put a dot in the middle of each segment also. Move the pin and ribbon to the bottom and repeat. Join up the dots top and bottom and draw in the circumference (*Figs.1 and 2*).

3. For the 7cm ball measure 4cm ($1^1/_2$") down from the top and 4cm up from the bottom and join up the dots. Do not mark in the circumference as the ball is too small for four rows (*Fig.3*).

4. Follow Design 1, steps 3–7, pages 14, 15 and 16 to cut the lines, make a ribbon hanging loop and cut and insert the fabric. For

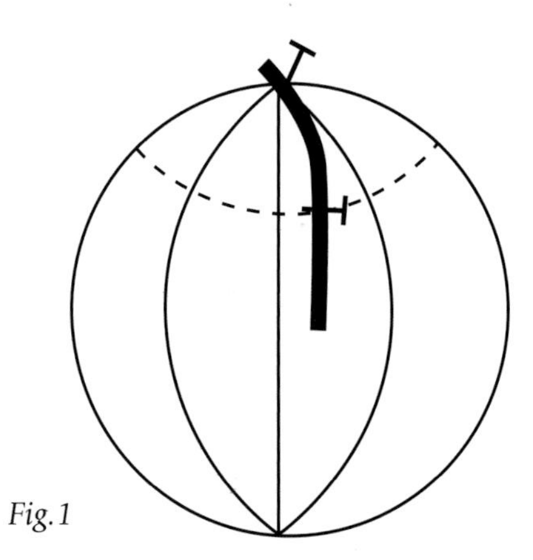
Fig.1

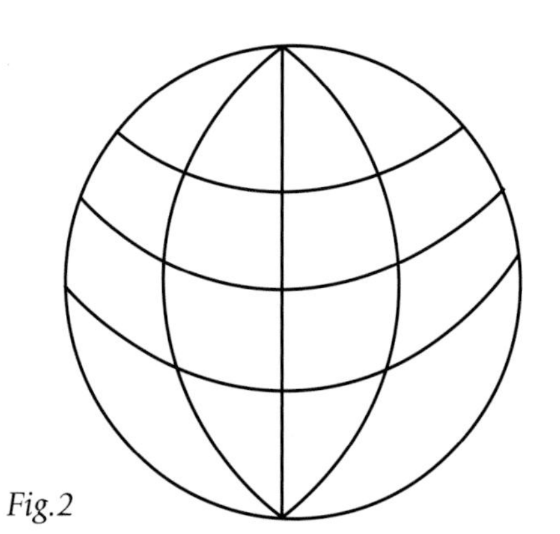
Fig.2

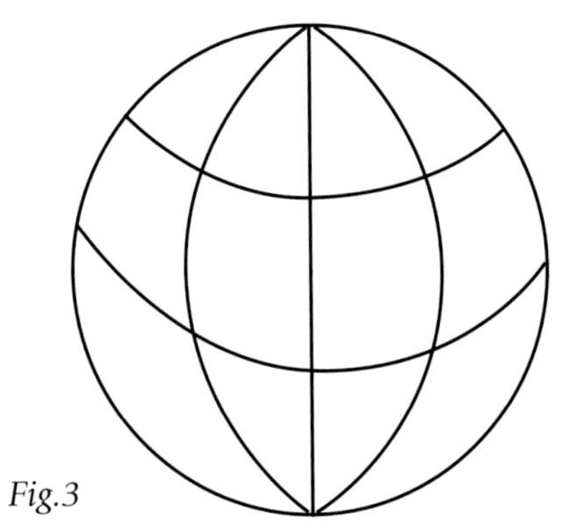
Fig.3

the 7cm ball choose soft fairly thin fabrics. For the 10cm ball I used four fabrics in two colours – a textured and smooth gold and a crushed and plain velvet. For the 12cm ball I used two fabrics. This is a good pattern for using up odd fragments of fabric.

5. After putting the fabric in place do the horizontal beading first. Where the two ends meet try to push the last bead down into the crack so that the vertical beading will lie smoothly over it. Do the vertical lines of beading last.

6. Finish off the balls following Design 1, steps 11–12, page 16.

Design No. 5 Chequered Ball

Ball	**7cm ball**	**10cm ball**	**12cm ball**
Two pieces of fabric each measuring	25cm x 21cm 10" x 8 1/2"	30cm x 30cm 12" x 12"	30cm x 35cm 12" x 14"
3mm gold ribbon	50cm (20")	60cm (2/3yd)	1m (1yd)
3mm beaded trim	1.30m (1 1/2yd)	2.25m (2 1/2yds)	2.75m (3yds)
Top finding + bottom decoration and short sequin pins			

Design No. 7 – Swirling Ball

Design No. 8 – Diamond Ball

Template 5

Template 5
12cm
10cm
7cm

DESIGN NO. 6
FLOWER BALL

Refer to the colour photograph page 27

I have called this the flower ball because of the sepals at the top.

1. Whichever sized ball you are using, mark the top and bottom and then divide the ball vertically into eight segments, marking the lines lightly. Design 1, steps 1–2, page 14.

2. Using a different coloured pen divide the 10cm and 12cm balls vertically again, so that you have 16 segments.

3. In this step you are creating the zigzag line around the top of each of the balls. To do this place an anchor pin near one end of a piece of ribbon.

a) For the 10cm ball: place another pin 3cm ($1\frac{1}{4}$") away and a third pin 5cm (2") away from the first pin.

b) For the 12cm ball: place another pin 4cm ($1\frac{1}{2}$") away and a third pin 7cm ($2\frac{3}{4}$") away from the first pin.
Push the anchor pin and ribbon into the top of the ball and make a mark on the original eighth segment lines at the 3cm pin for the 10cm ball (4cm for the 12cm ball) and then make a dot on the second coloured (sixteenth) set of lines at 5cm for the 10cm ball (7cm for the 12cm ball). *Fig.1*. Join up the dots (*Fig.2*).

c) For a 7cm ball which is only divided into eighths, place a marker pin 3cm ($\frac{1}{4}$") away from the anchor pin on a piece of ribbon and another pin 5cm (2") from the anchor pin. Push the anchor pin and ribbon into the top of the ball and make a mark on the eighth segment line where the 3cm pin crosses the line. Make a mark in *between* the segment lines at the 5cm (2") pin. Join up the dots.

4. In this step you are creating the zigzag line that goes around the base of the ball – this is done on the 10 and 12 cm balls only. Make a dot on the circumference where each of the first set of vertical lines cross. This will be the point of the zigzag.

5. Using the ribbon as a measure, place a pin marker 10.5cm or $4\frac{1}{2}$" from the anchor pin for the 10cm ball (13.5cm $5\frac{1}{2}$" from the anchor pin for the 12cm ball). Turn the ball so that the bottom is now the top and pin the ribbon to the top. Using the pin as a guide make a dot on the second, coloured, set of lines as in *Fig.3*. Join up the dots. The 7cm ball does not need this stage.

6. With so many lines on your ball, check that you know which are going to be the cutting lines and if necessary go over them in a heavier pen following the pattern on *Fig.4*.

7. Cut the ball, pierce and make a hanging loop making sure that the loop end comes out at the 'sepal' top. If you want to add a hanging decoration do so now. (For detailed instructions on

doing this refer to Design 1, step 6, page 15.)

8. Start by putting in the material for the sepals, then the large middle petals and lastly the bottom row.

9. Pin the beaded trim around the sepals first following the zigzag line. Secure the trim at the top and bottom of each point. Pin the bottom zigzag line in place in the same way. Starting at the top of the bottom zigzag run a line of beading up through the sepal, across the top of the ball, ending at the top of the bottom zigzag on the opposite side of the ball. Lastly put on the beading for the bottom section, running the beading from the bottom point of the zigzag across the base and up to the bottom point of the zigzag opposite. This is the order I work in but you can put the beadings in place whichever way you choose.

10. Finish off in the usual way see Design 1, steps 11–12, page 16 for more detailed instructions.

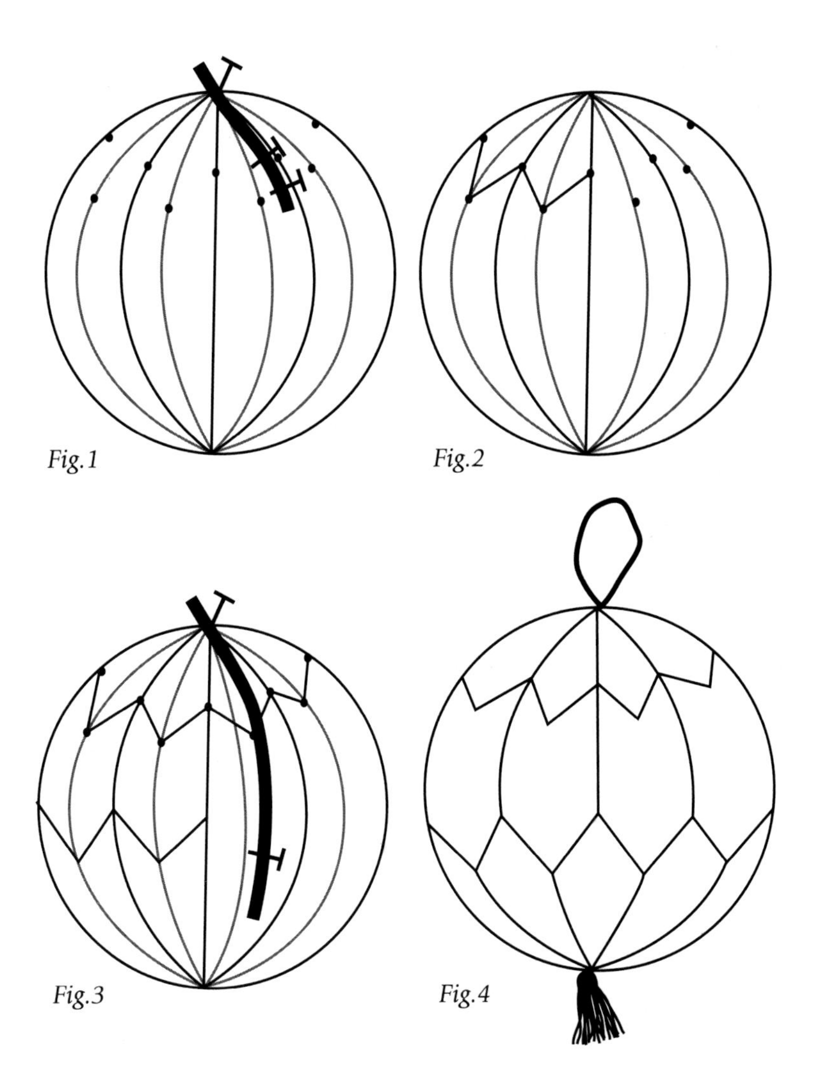

Design No. 6 – Flower Ball

Ball	7cm ball	10cm ball	12cm ball
Fabric –sepals	21 x 17cm (8 x 7")	22 x 19cm (9 x 8")	27 x 21cm (11 x 8")
Fabric – middle	25 x 22cm (10 x 9")	35 x 22cm (14 x 9")	35 x 25cm (14 x 10")
Fabric – bottom	-	30 x 23cm (12 x 9")	30 x 24cm (12 x 10")
3mm gold ribbon	50cm (20")	60cm (3/4yd)	1m (1yd)
3mm beaded trim	1.35m (1 1/2yds)	2m (2 1/4yds)	2.75m (3yds)
Top finding + bottom decoration and short sequin pins			

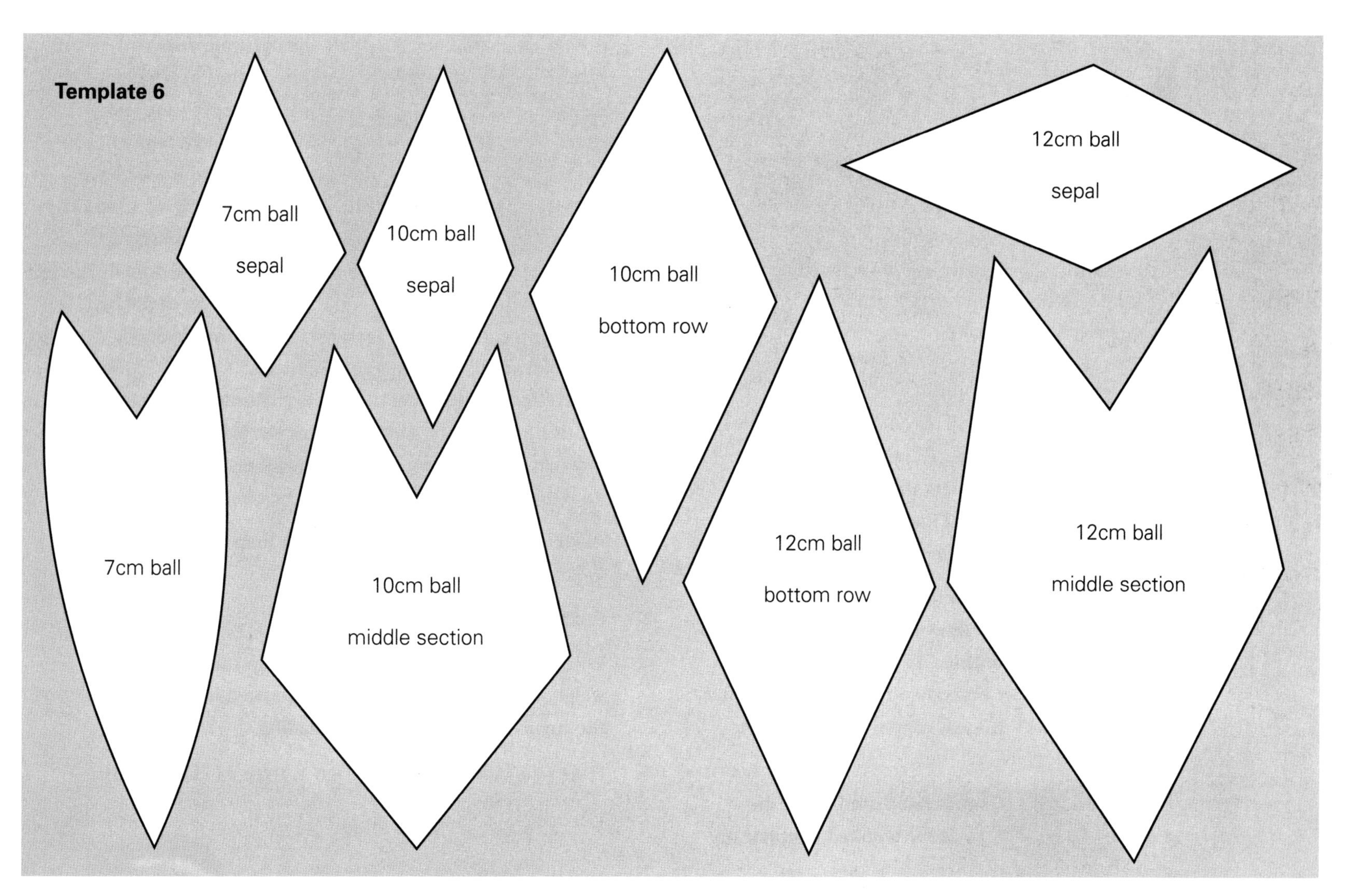
Template 6
7cm ball
sepal
10cm ball
sepal
10cm ball
bottom row
12cm ball
sepal
7cm ball
10cm ball
middle section
12cm ball
bottom row
12cm ball
middle section

DESIGN NO. 7
SWIRLING BALL

Refer to the colour photographs page 30

This makes a wonderful bauble and looks spectacular on the larger balls. I divide the 7cm ball into eighths, 10cm ball into twelfths and the 12cm ball into sixteenths. Choose fabrics which are stretchy or have some give in them. If in doubt cut out a piece of fabric and try it. If you have difficulty test out another fabric.

7cm Ball

1. Mark the top and bottom of the ball. Lay a piece of 3mm ribbon around the ball but instead of marking the vertical segment lines in one continuous line, just mark them with dots. Make sure you put a dot where the vertical line crosses the circumference. (*Fig.1*). Then you have two choices:

a) Starting from the circumference where a vertical segment line crosses the circumference, lightly draw a biro line in a curve from the middle to the top. Continue all around the top half (*Fig.2*). Turn the ball the other way up and do a curve the other way (*Fig.3*). I find it is easier this way than to try and do one long curve.

b) If drawing a free hand curve is somewhat daunting use the templates given see *Template 7*. Trace the required template on to thin paper and cut out. Mark the circumference end on the pattern with 'c'. Line up the biro dot on the circumference with the end of the template at the point marked 'c', and the straighter edge of the template along the dotted segment line. Pin the template in place and make a mark on it where the curved line touches the dotted segment line (*Fig.4*). Check that the template has not increased in size in the reproduction process. The traced pattern must not overlap the dotted segment lines, if it does trim it. Draw the curved line on to the ball. Do all the top curves first. Then turn the ball upside down, turn the template around and repeat the process.
Check that the divisions along the circumference line look relatively equal as it is the centre of the ball which will show most. By the time you have put the fabrics in and the beading on minor variations will not show.

2. Pierce the ball and insert the ribbon loop see Design 1, steps 4–6, pages 14 and 15.

3. Cut the lines you have marked.

4. When applying the fabrics remember to start with the lightest weight fabric first. You may find you need to use extra pins on the curves when attaching the beading.

5. Finish the ball following Design 1, steps 11–12, page 16.

10cm Ball Divided into Twelfths

1. Mark the top and bottom of the ball. Divide the ball into half using the piece of ribbon and make a series of dots along the vertical segment lines. Divide each half into three by marking biro dots 5.25cm (2 1/16") away from each other along the circumference line as described in Design 3, step 2, page 22. Then divide these segments into half again.
2. Now mark on the curved lines. Draw free hand or use the curve of the template given (*Template 7*). Draw as described for the 7cm ball above.
3. Continue as for the 7cm ball, remembering to add a hanging decoration, if using one, to the loop. The 4mm faceted trim looks particularly good on this and the 12cm ball.

12cm Ball Divided into Sixteenths

I find it much easier to divide a ball into sixteenths rather than twelfths. Follow the instructions given with Design 1, steps 1–2, page 14 then divide each segment into half so that you have 16 segments. Mark the sixteenths with biro dots and use the curved template given (*Template 7*) or draw freehand. Continue as above.

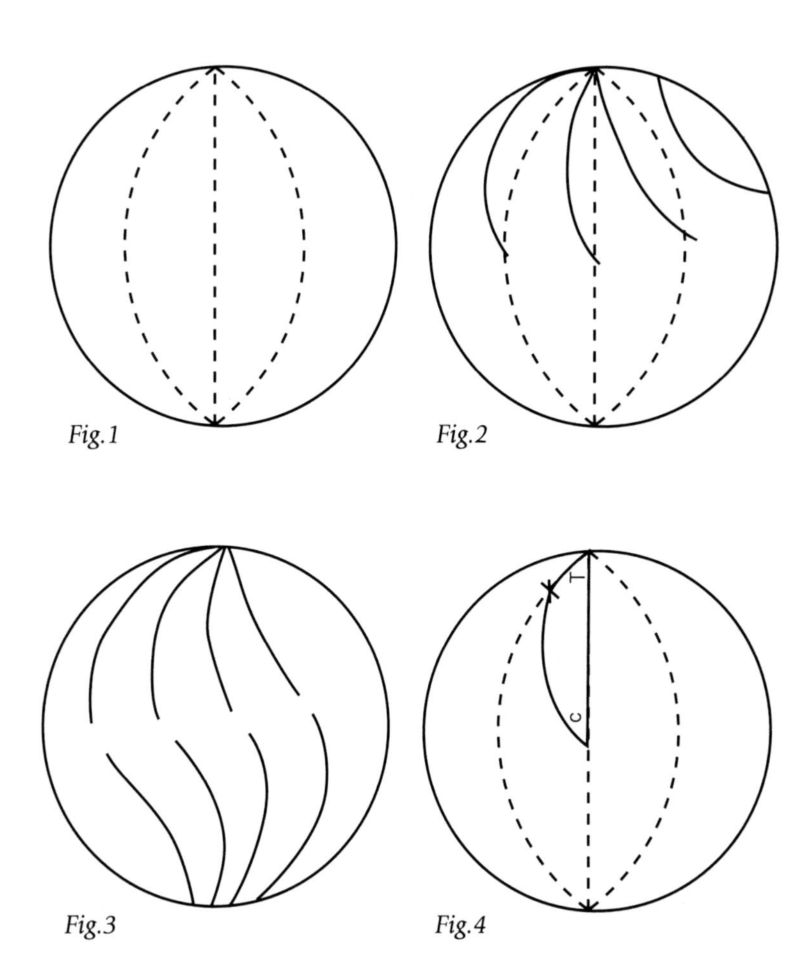

Fig.1 *Fig.2* *Fig.3* *Fig.4*

Design No. 7 – Swirling Ball

Ball	7cm ball	10cm ball	12cm ball
Two pieces of fabric each measuring	28cm x 15cm 11" x 6"	30cm x 18cm 12" x 7 1/2"	40cm x 21cm 16" x 8 1/2"
3mm gold ribbon	50cm (20")	60cm (2/3yd)	1m (1yd)
Beaded trim	3mm – 1m (1 1/4yds)	4mm –2.50m (2 1/2yds)	4mm – 3.50m (3 1/2yds)
Top finding + bottom decoration and short sequin pins			

Template 7

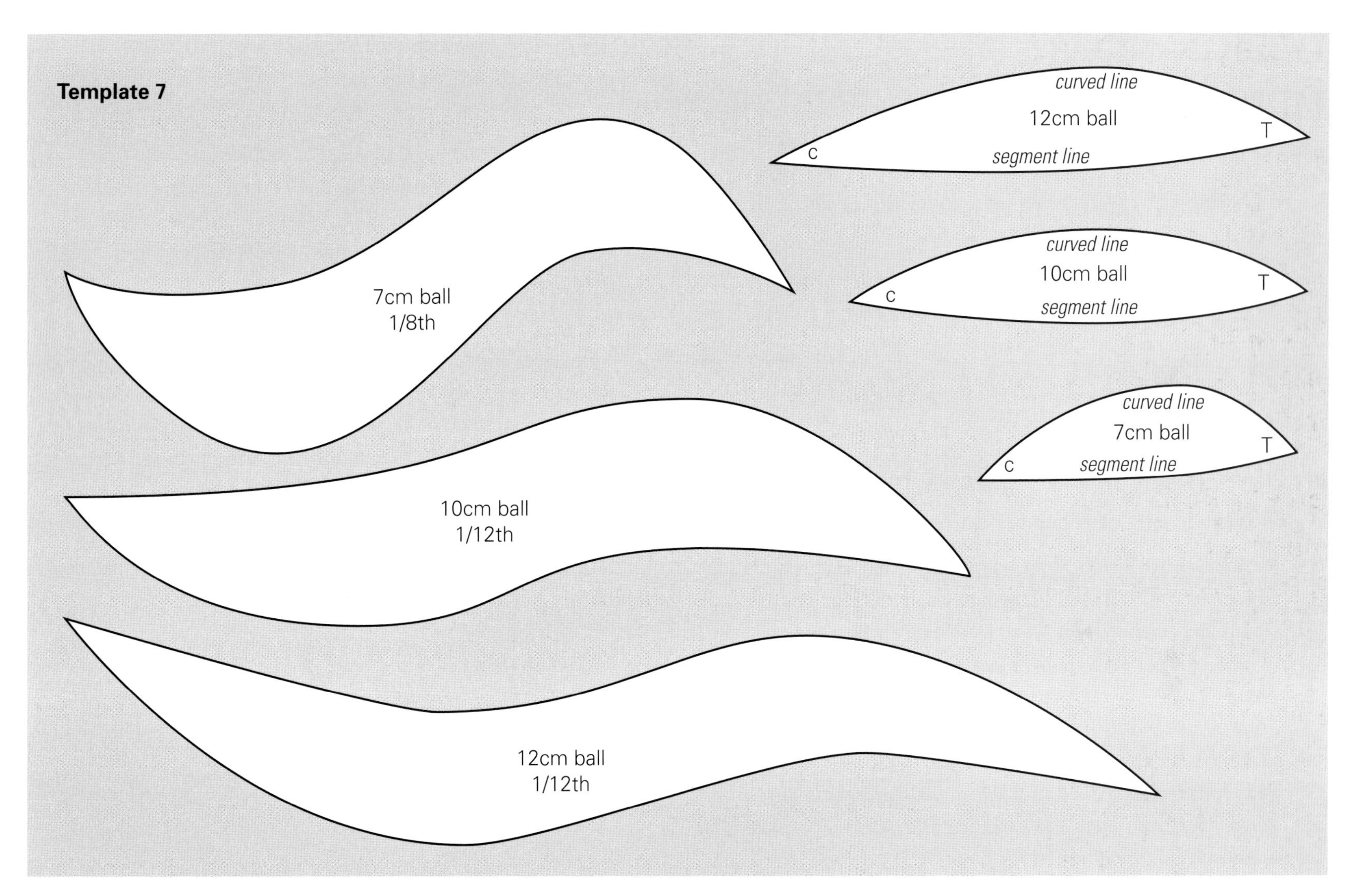

curved line
12cm ball
T
C
segment line
curved line
10cm ball
T
C
segment line
curved line
7cm ball
T
C
segment line
7cm ball
1/8th
10cm ball
1/12th
12cm ball
1/12th

DESIGN NO. 8
DIAMOND BALL

Refer to the colour photograph page 31

This bauble has a line of diamonds around the middle and works well on balls of all sizes.

1. Mark the top and bottom of the ball and divide the ball (size 7, 10 or 12cm) into eighths following Design 1, steps 1–2, page 14, trying to be as accurate as possible.

2. Place an anchor pin near one end of a piece of ribbon:

a) for the 7cm ball place another pin 2.75cm ($1^1/_8$") away

b) for the 10cm ball place another pin 3cm ($1^1/_4$") away

c) for the 12cm ball place another pin 5cm (2") away.

3. To mark the top and bottom points of the diamond push the anchor pin and ribbon into the ball where the segment line crosses the circumference (*Fig.1*). Swing the ribbon up and make a biro dot at the point where the pin lies half way between the segments above the circumference line and then do the same below. Swing the ribbon around and do the same for the adjacent segment. Move the anchor pin to the next segment line and repeat. Join up the dots between the segments to the point where the circumference and segment lines cross to form a diamond. Do this all round the ball (*Fig.1*).

4. Cut the ball and insert the hanging loop (See Design 1, steps 3–6, pages 14 and 15).

5. Start by putting the fabric in the middle row of diamonds. You can use a wide range of fabrics. For the 7cm ball I have used two similar fabrics but for the 10cm ball I have contrasted velvet with a glittery fabric. For the 12cm ball I like to use a fabric made up of sequined dots as this adds interest to a fairly large diamond.

6. On the 10cm ball I have used a flat braid for a change. There is no right or wrong way to put the braid or beading on. One way is to start at the top of the ball down a vertical segment line, then branch off down the side of one diamond, continuing in a straight line down the side of the next diamond and back on to the segment line. If you do that all around first you just have one line down the sides of the diamonds to do last.

7. Finish off in the usual way: See Design 1, steps 11–12, page 16 for detailed instructions.

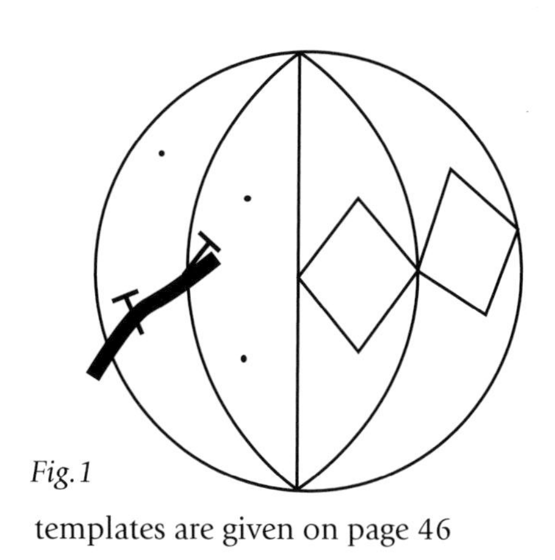

Fig. 1

templates are given on page 46

Design No. 8 – Diamond Ball

Ball	7cm ball	10cm ball	12cm ball
Fabric 1 – for top and bottom	25cm x 36cm 10" x 14"	24cm x 45cm 9 1/2" x 18"	30cm x 50cm 12" x 19"
Fabric 2 - for central diamond	15cm x 24cm 6" x 9 1/2"	25cm x 20cm 10" x 8"	30cm x 25cm 12" x 10"
3mm gold ribbon	50cm (20")	60cm (2/3yd)	1m (1yd)
3mm beaded trim	1.50m (1 2/3yd)	2.25m (2 1/3yd)	2.50m (2 2/3yd)
Top finding + bottom decoration. Short sequin pins			

Design No. 9 – Multi Diamond Ball

Design No. 10 – Circles

Template 8

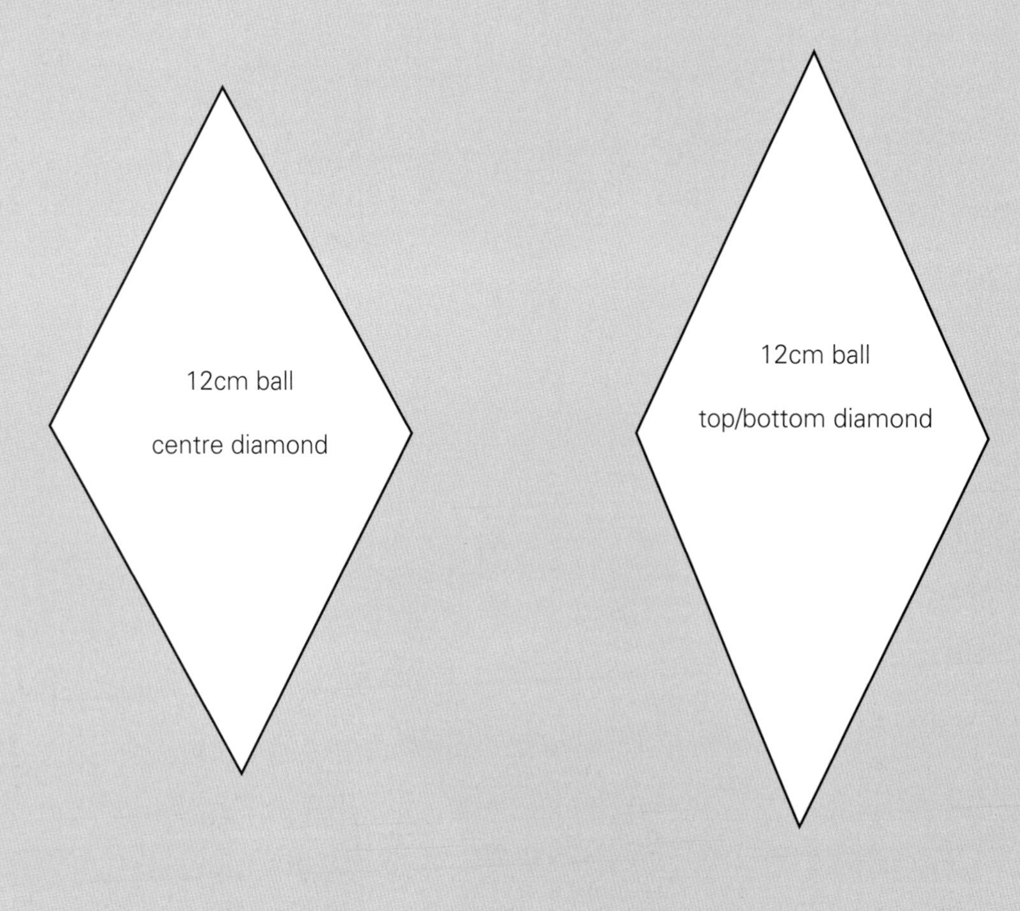

Template 8

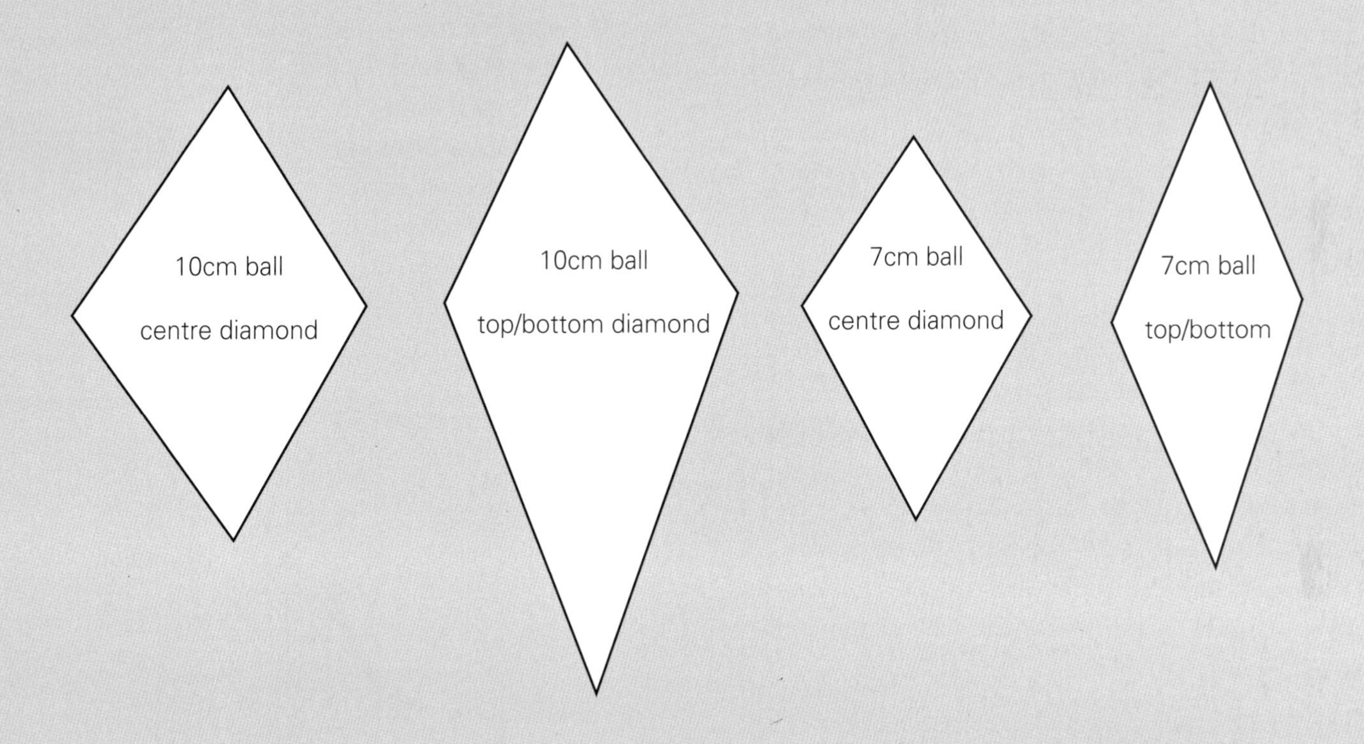
10cm ball
centre diamond
10cm ball
top/bottom diamond
7cm ball
centre diamond
7cm ball
top/bottom

DESIGN NO. 9
MULTI DIAMOND BALL

Refer to the colour photograph page 44

Use a 10cm or 12cm ball for this design, as I find a 7cm ball is just not big enough. Because the individual diamonds are small I have used fabrics which are similar and not thick, e.g. mirror lamé in red, green and gold.

1. Mark the top and bottom and divide the ball into eighths following Design 1, steps 1–2, page 14.
2. Place an anchor pin near one end of a piece of ribbon:

a) for the 10cm ball place another pin 2.5cm ($1^1/_8$") away

b) for the 12 cm ball place another pin 3.5cm ($1^3/_8$") away

3. To start marking the diamonds push in the anchor pin where the circumference crosses a vertical segment line and make a dot half way between the segments, above the circumference and also below (see Design 8, step 3, page 42). Join up the dots between the segments to the point where the circumference and segment lines cross to form a diamond. Do this all round the ball (*Fig.1*, page 43)
4. Next take the anchor pin to the top of the diamond and mark where the ribbon crosses the segment line, working up from the central diamonds. Join up these dots (*Fig.1*). Turn the ball upside down and repeat, making another row of diamonds. On completion there are three rows of central diamonds then a further row of diamonds top and bottom.
5. Cut the ball and insert the hanging loop (see Design 1, steps 3–4, page 14).
6. To follow my colour scheme you will need:
   4 red central diamonds
   4 green central diamonds
   16 gold central diamond
   8 red top/bottom diamonds
   8 green top/bottom diamonds

Fig.1

Start by putting in the middle row, along the circumference, alternating red and green. Next put the red and green top/bottom diamonds in place and finally the gold.

7. For an additional decorative feature which adds more sparkle and interest you can place a gold bead on to a small sequin and bead pin and push it into the angles of the diamonds.

8. Finish the balls in the usual way following Design 1, steps 11–12, page 16.

Design No. 9 – Multi-Diamond Ball

Ball	**10cm ball**	**12cm ball**
Fabric – red	24 x 23cm (9½" x 9")	28 x 28cm (11" x 11")
Fabric – green	24 x 23cm (9½" x 9")	28 x 28cm (11" x 11")
Fabric – gold	24 x 26cm (9½" x 10")	28 x 24cm (11" x 9½")
3mm gold ribbon	60cm (⅔yd)	1m (1yd)
3mm beaded trim	2.50m (2¾yds)	3m (3¼yds)

Top finding and corsage or hat pin + bead for bottom. Short sequin pins

Template 9

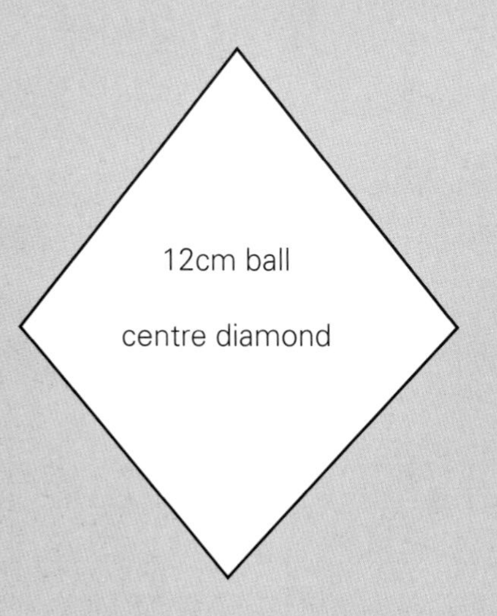

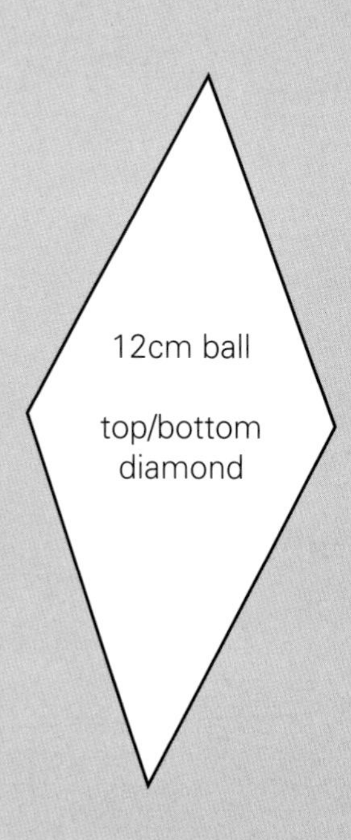

Template 9

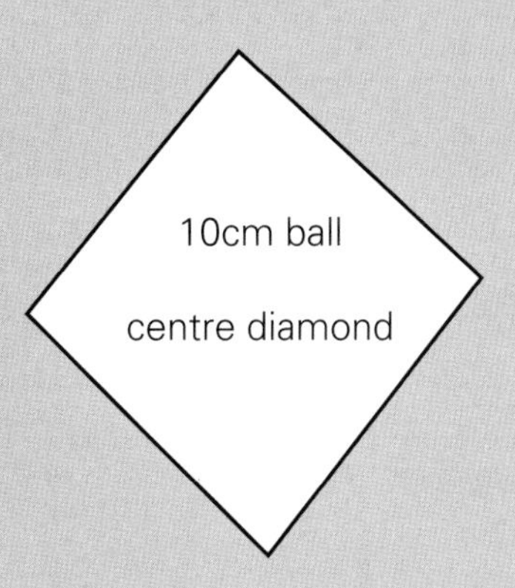

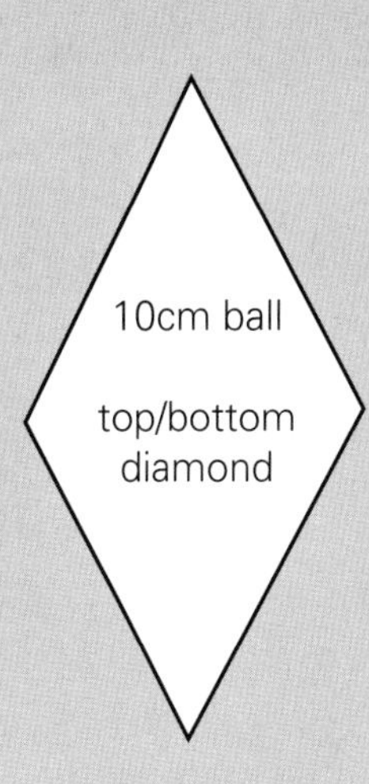

DESIGN NO. 10
CIRCLES

Refer to the colour photograph page 45

The instructions for this design are for a 10cm ball only, it would also work on a 12cm ball but the 7cm ball is too small. The design uses circles which are a little more difficult to work than straight lines. Choose a soft, malleable material for making the circle.

1. Take a 10cm ball and mark the top and bottom. Divide the ball into eighths following the instructions given in Design 1, steps 1–2, page 14.

2. In order to make a line of circles that touch each other but do not overlap, each circle needs to be a little smaller than the width of the segment at the circumference. There are at least two ways of marking these circles. If your ball has accurate eighths marked on it by the manufacturer you can draw a circle with a diameter of 3.7cm ($1\frac{1}{2}$") using the template given (*Template 10*, page 58). This is less than the actual width of the segment of 4.38cm ($1\frac{3}{4}$"). Draw around the template, cut out the tracing, check that the circle has not got any bigger in the process then centre the template over the circumference and vertical segment lines and mark the circle on the ball.
   Alternatively put a pin in the end of a piece of ribbon and another marker pin 1.8cm ($\frac{11}{16}$") along. Push the anchor pin down into the ball where the segment line crosses the circumference and make a series of dots in a circle (*Fig.1*). Move the anchor pin to the next segment/circumference crossing. The next circle should almost touch the last. If it overlaps your segment line is out. You need to leave a little space, say 2mm or $\frac{1}{16}$", between circles to allow for the fabric to be pushed in and for the beading.

3. Mark all the circles and cut them. Then cut the segment lines from the top of the circles to the top of the ball and the bottom of the circle to the bottom of the ball.

4. Insert the hanging loop and any decoration to hang from the base of the ball, following Design 1, step 6, page 15.

5. Start by putting the fabric over the circles and push it in. If the material keeps coming out push a small pin down into the crack to stabilise it. Then do the other shapes.

6. For the beading put the segment lines in first and then you can go around the circles in a continuous wavy line (*Fig.2*).

7. Finish the ball by following Design 1, steps 11–12, page 16.

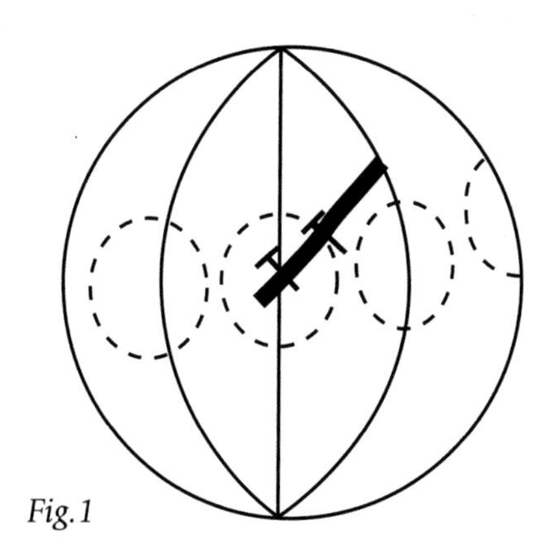

Fig.1

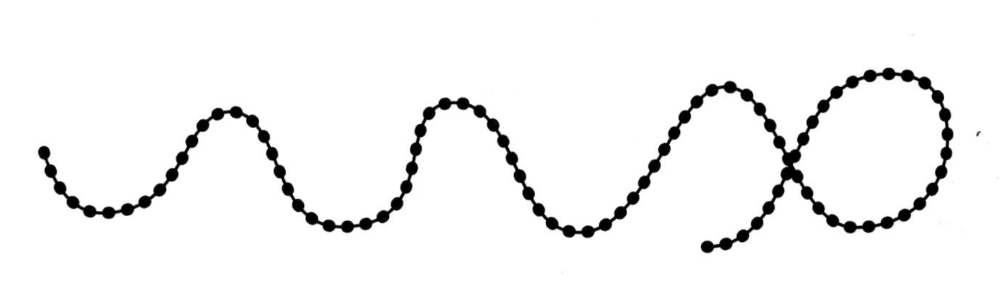

Fig.2

Design No. 10 – Circles

Ball	**10cm ball**
Fabric for circles	25 x 15cm (10" x 6")
Fabric for top and bottom	25 x 45cm (10" x 18")
3mm gold ribbon	60cm (2/3yd)
3mm beaded trim	2.25m (2 1/3yds)
Top finding, hanging decoration and short pins	

DESIGN NO. 11
CIRCLES WITHIN CIRCLES

Refer to the colour photograph page 57

You can do this on any size ball. I have varied the design by having circles within circles on the 7cm and 10cm balls and a Christmas tree on the 12cm ball. When selecting the fabric for the circles choose a thin fabric or one with lots of 'give'.

1. Start by marking the top and bottom.
2. Divide the ball into four quarters vertically marking the lines lightly or using a disappearing pen if you have one.
3. Using a piece of narrow ribbon and two pins as markers, measure the distance along the circumference of one quarter (*Fig.1*). Fold the ribbon in half between the pins and place a third pin in the middle. Push this middle pin right down into the ball where the circumference line crosses a quarter line. Move *one* of the other pins *fractionally towards the middle pin* and use *this pin* as a marker. Swing the pin and ribbon around in a circle making a series of small marks. Then do the other three circles. They should *almost* touch, say 2mm or 1/16" apart (*Fig.2*).
4. To make a circle within this circle (for the 7cm and 10cm balls) fold the ribbon in half between the centre pin and an outside pin and place a marker on the fold. Push this pin into the cross formed by the circumference and quarter line and mark another circle (*Fig.3*).
5. Join up all the marks and cut the circles. Then cut the quarter lines from the top of the ball to the top of the circle and from the bottom of the ball to the bottom of the circle. Do not cut the quarter lines within the circles.
6. Insert the hanging loop following Design 1, steps 4–5, pages 14 and 15.
7. Then put the fabrics in place, using fairly thin fabrics with a bit of stretch or give for the circles. Start by putting the largest circle in place first. Cut out a piece of fabric large enough to cover the whole circle and work around the outer edges. For the 7cm and 10cm balls make a snip in the centre of the fabric circle and cut away sufficient fabric to allow you to push the fabric down into the inner circle. You now have an outer ring. Next place a small piece of fabric over the central remaining circle and push the edges down into the crack. If you have any difficulty or the fabric tries to escape you can tether it with some short pins. These will be covered up by the beading later. Finally put the background fabric in place.
8. On the 12cm ball instead of putting in a second circle I used ribbon to make a Christmas tree. To do this you will need 1m (1 yd) of ribbon about 25mm (1") wide.

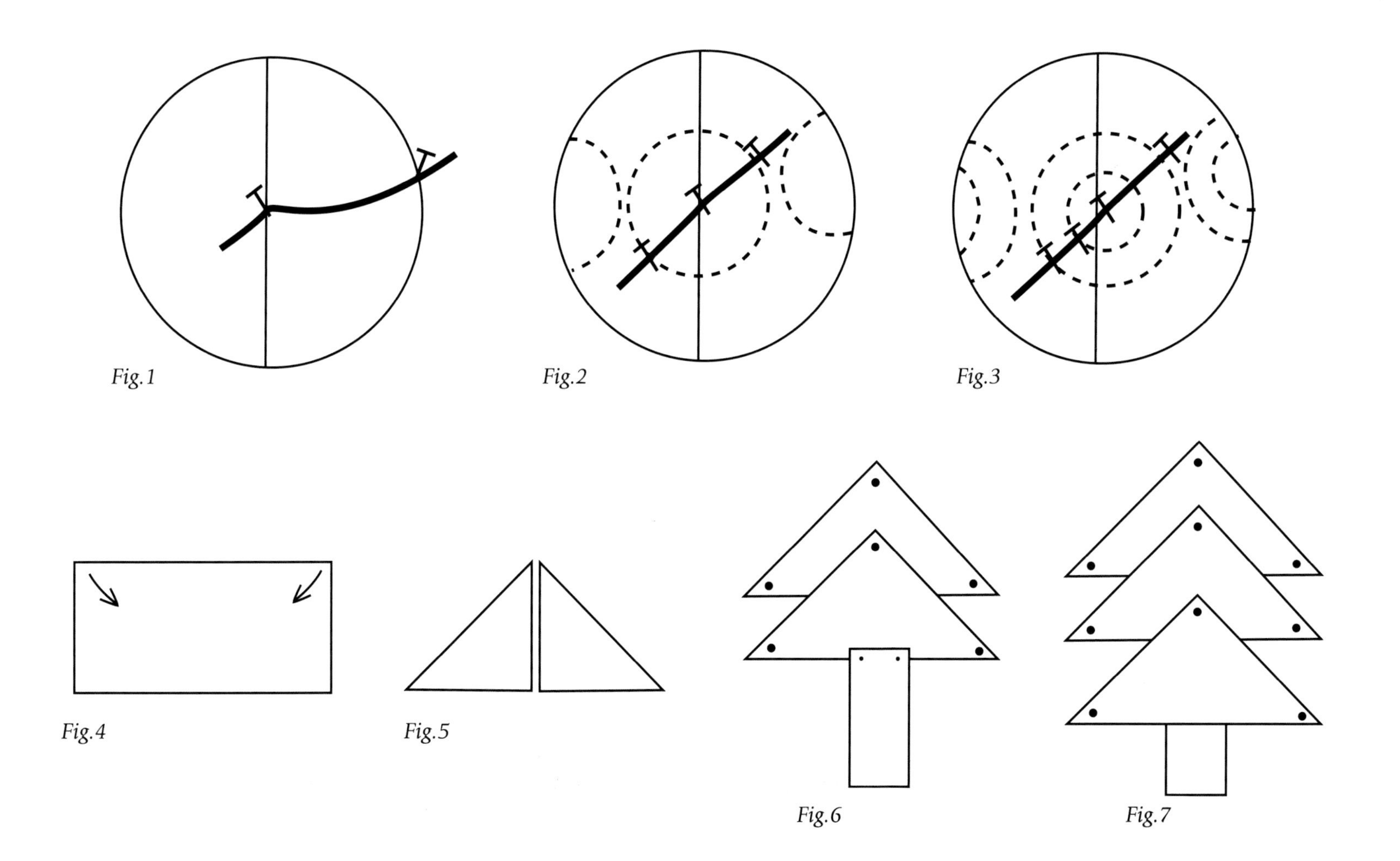
Fig.1
Fig.2
Fig.3
Fig.4
Fig.5
Fig.6
Fig.7

To make the triangles, cut the ribbon into 12 rectangles double the width of the ribbon. Fold the rectangles into triangles and crease the fold with your fingernail (*Figs.4 and 5*). Pin the top two triangles in place on the ball using a bead or sequin on a small pin. To make the tree trunk cut 4 pieces of ribbon 3cm (1 1/4") long and fold the two ends into the middle. Pin this, overlapping the second triangle and tucking a second pin into the fold at the bottom of the trunk (*Fig.6*). Then put the third triangle in place with a beaded pin (*Fig.7*).

9. Apply the beaded trim to the vertical quarter lines first then do the circles, refer back to Design 10, *Fig.2*, page 53.
10. Finish the ball following Design 1, steps 11–12, page 16.

Design No. 11 – Circles within Circles

Ball	7mm ball	10cm ball	12cm ball
Fabric – small circle	10 x 10cm (4" x 4")	15 x 15cm (6" x 6")	–
Fabric – outer circle	15 x 15cm (6"x 6")	20cm x 20cm (8" x 8")	25 x 25cm (10" x 10")
Fabric – top/bottom	25 x 18cm (10" x 7")	30 x 26cm (12" x 10")	36 x 24cm (14" x 10")
3mm gold ribbon	50cm (20")	60cm (2/3yd)	1m (1yd)
3mm beaded trim	1.25m (1 1/3yds)	1.75m (2yds)	2.50m (2 2/3yds)
25mm ribbon (1")	–	–	1m (1yd)
Top finding + corsage or hat pins and beads. Short pins			

Design No. 11 – Circles Within Circles

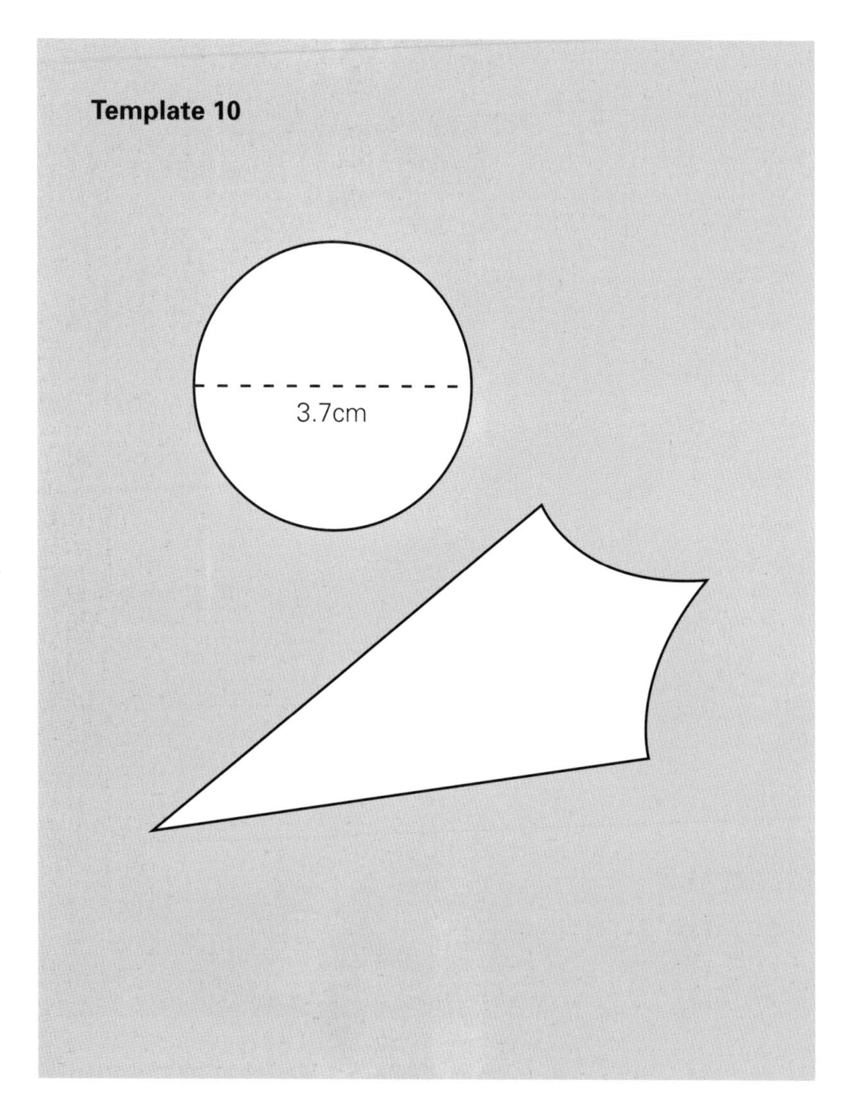
Template 10
3.7cm

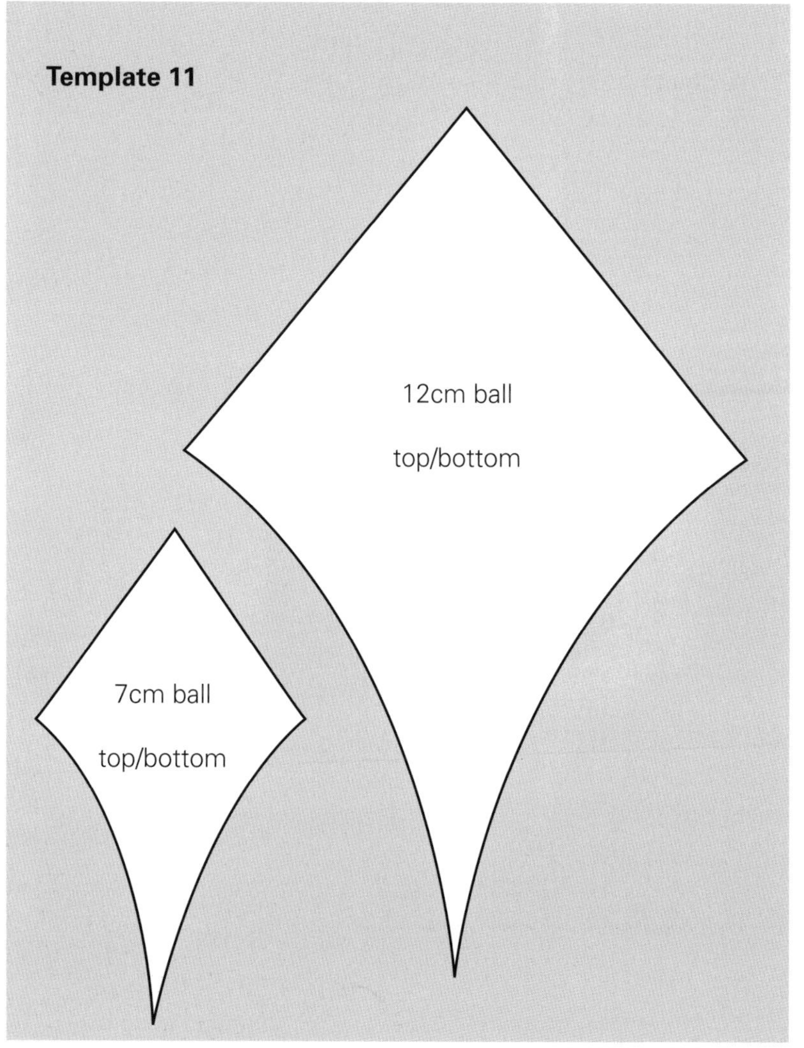
Template 11
12cm ball
top/bottom
7cm ball
top/bottom

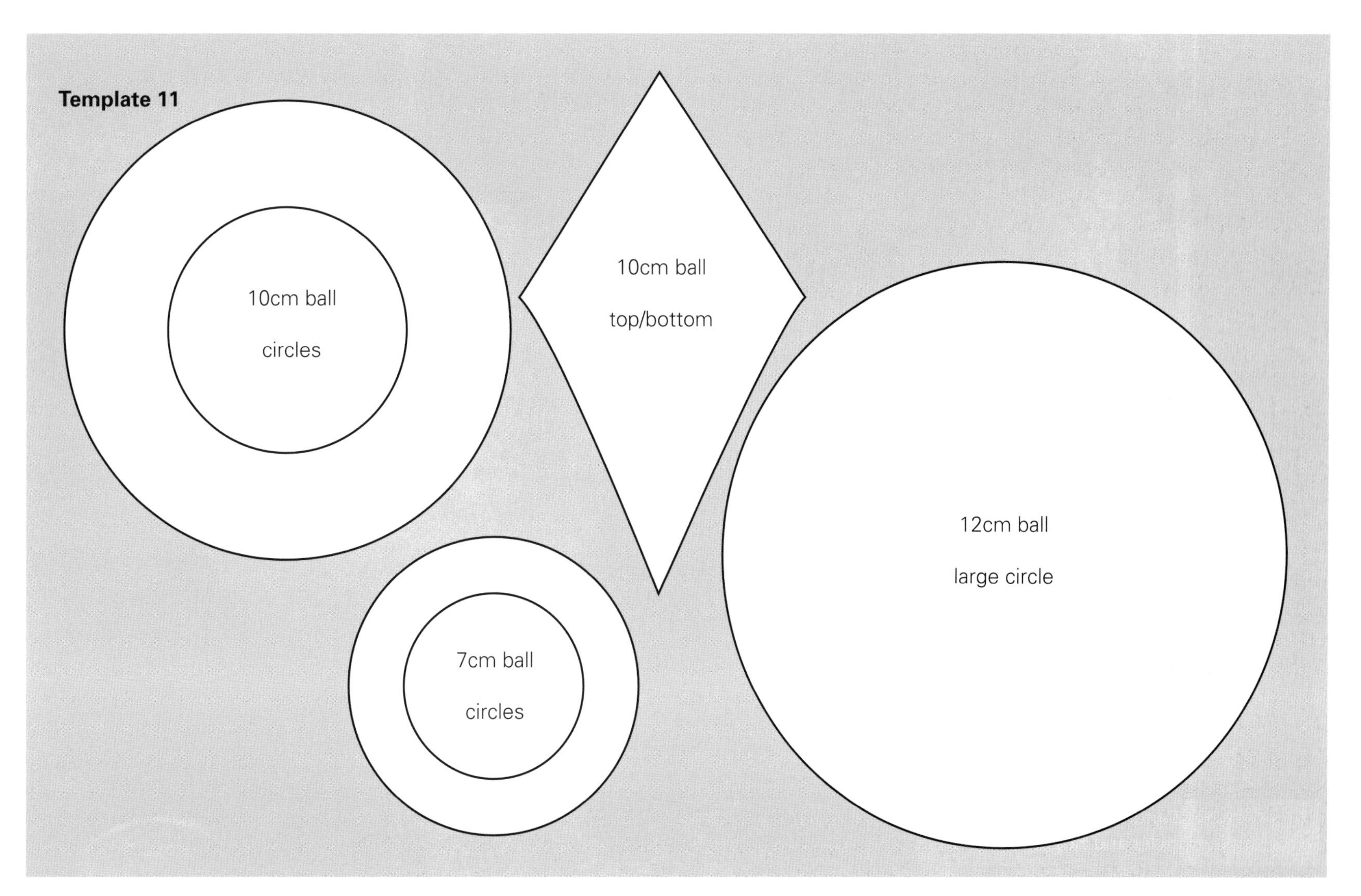
Template 11
10cm ball
circles
10cm ball
top/bottom
12cm ball
large circle
7cm ball
circles

Design Nos. 12 and 14 –
Overlapping Circles and Brighton Pavilion

Design No. 13 – The Balloon Ball

DESIGN NO. 12
OVERLAPPING CIRCLES

Refer to the colour photograph page 60

Continuing with the theme of circles, I have made a row of overlapping circles, using a 12cm ball so as not to make it all too fiddly. I used soft malleable fabrics for the circles – a red sequin dot plus a plain gold, with a red velvet for the top and bottom of the ball

1. Mark the top and bottom. Lightly mark in eight segments (see Design 1, steps 1–2, page 14).
2. Using a piece of thin ribbon measure the distance along the circumference line between two vertical segment lines and mark the distance with two pins. Fold the ribbon in half between the two pins and place a third pin in the middle.
3. Push the pin at one end into the point where the circumference and a segment line cross. Using the pin at the other end make a series of dots in an extended semi-circle (*Fig.1*).
4. Use the middle pin to mark the middle point between the segment lines on the circumference and push the first pin in at this mark and make another extended semi-circle (*Fig.2*). Do this all around until you have 16 semi-circles (*Fig.3*). Join up the dots.
5. Cut the curved lines you have marked. At the top cut four quarter lines and do the same at the bottom.
6. Insert the ribbon loop with a hanging decoration and put the fabrics in place. Following Design 1, steps 4–6, pages 14 and 15.
7. Cut the fabric out using the templates given, remember to cut the fabric out 1cm (3/8") bigger than the templates on each side.
8. Insert the fabric semi-circles using the thinner, where applicable, of the two fabrics first – in my case the red sequin dot. When the semi-circles are in place put in the fabric at the top and bottom.
9. I found the best way of putting on the beading was to do each extended semi-circle individually, then put in the quarter vertical lines at the top and bottom of the ball.
10. Finish the ball in the usual way, see Design 1, steps 11–12, page 16.

Design No. 12 – Overlapping Circles

Ball	12cm ball
Two pieces of fabric for the semi-circles each measuring	32 x 26cm (12 1/2" x 10")
Fabric for top/bottom	30 x 15cm (12" x 6")
3mm gold ribbon	1m (1yd)
3mm beaded trim	3m (3 1/3yds)
Top finding + hanging decoration and short pins	

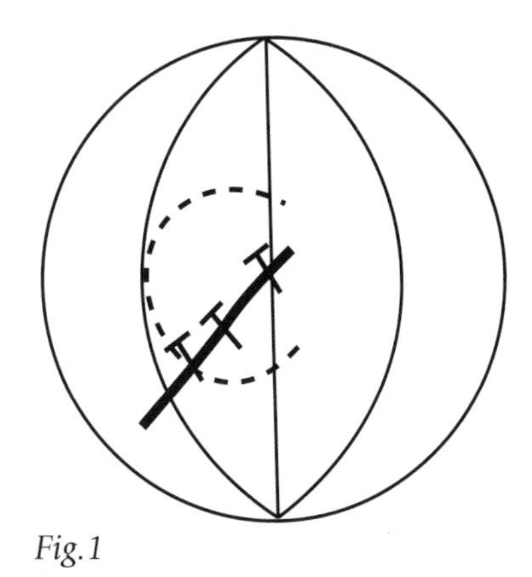

Fig.1

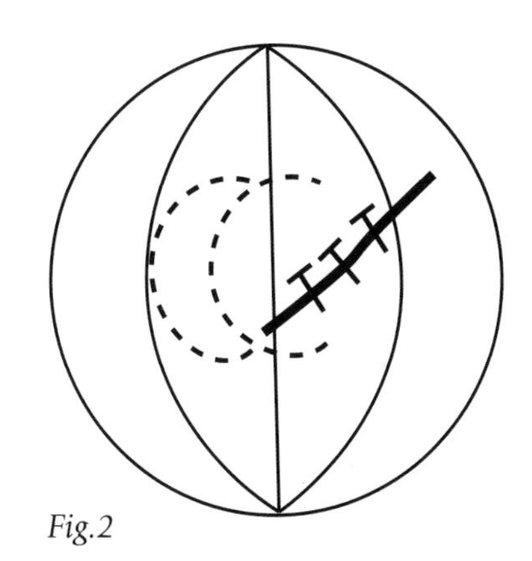

Fig.2

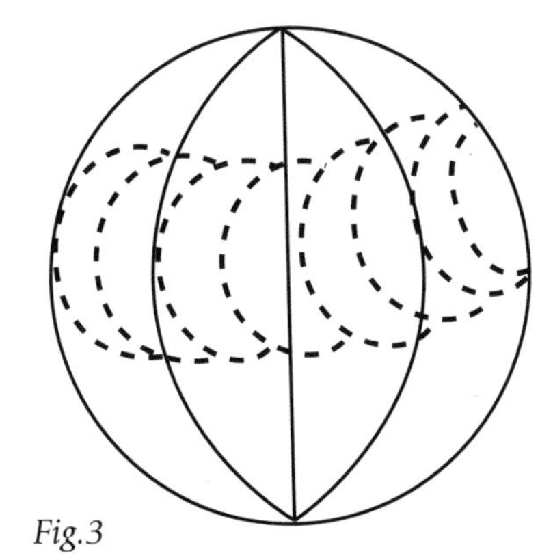

Fig.3

Design Nos. 15 and 16 –
Folded and Pleated Ribbon Balls

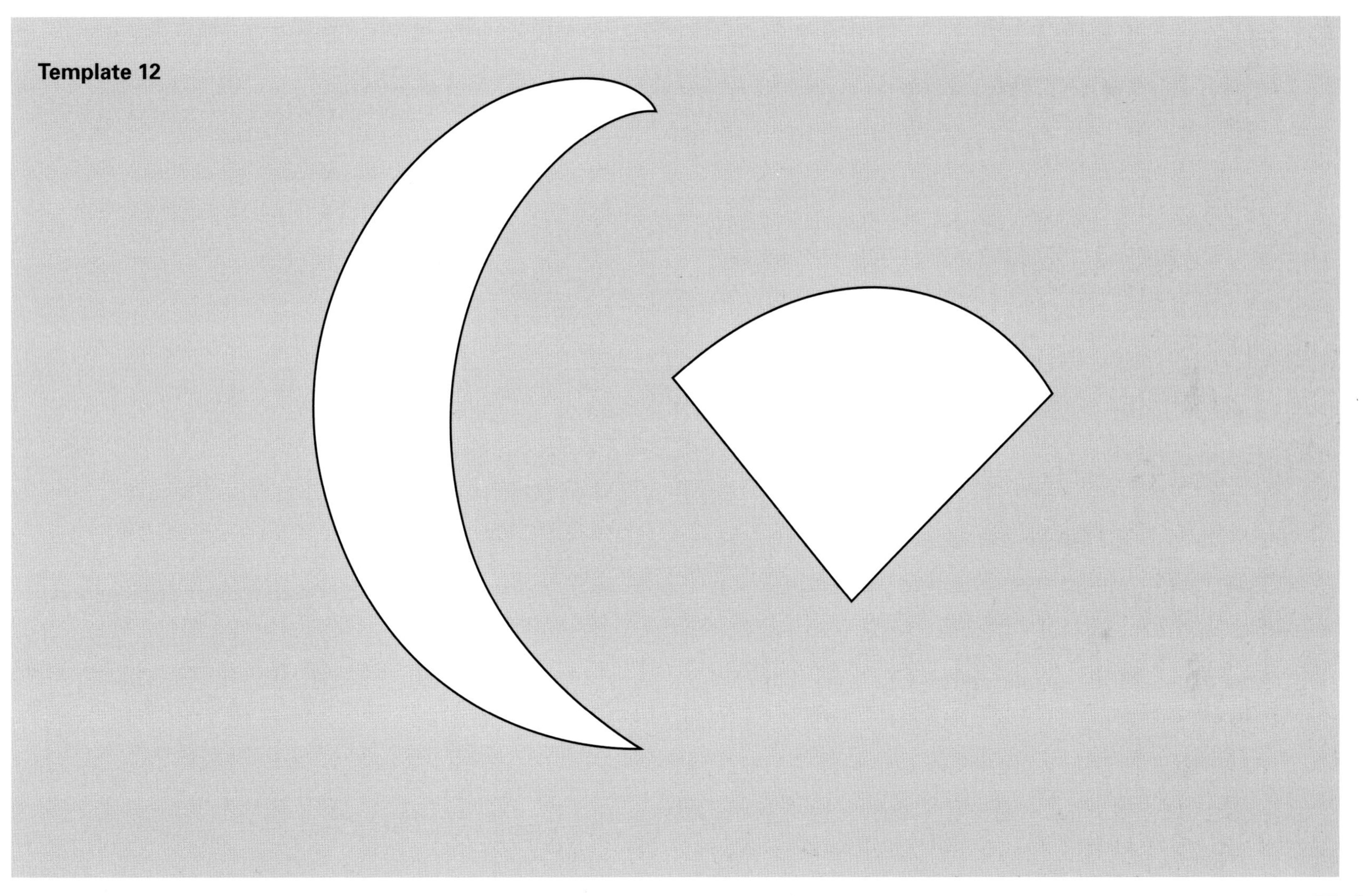
Template 12

DESIGN NO. 13
THE BALLOON BALL

Refer to the colour photograph page 61

This design, reminiscent of a hot air balloon, is great for using up scraps of fabrics. You can make it in any size, just altering the number of bands of colour. It takes a bit of time to draw and cut the pattern. Use a selection of soft pliable fabrics for the zigzag sections.

1. Mark the top and bottom of the ball making sure you know which is which.

2. Lightly mark in eight segment lines (Design 1, step 2, page 14).

3. **For the 7cm Ball:**

a) Place an anchor pin near one end of a piece of ribbon and another pin 4.5cm (1 3/4") away then place two more pins 1.5cm (5/8") apart.

b) Push the first anchor pin into the top of the ball and lay the ribbon along a vertical (eighth) segment line. Make marks where the pins cross the line, repeat on each of the eighth segment lines (*Fig.1*).

c) Remove the marker pins.

d) Use the ribbon to divide the eighths in half, using a different coloured pen, so that you now have sixteen vertical segment lines. These latest lines are referred to as 'sixteenth' lines.

e) Put the first anchor pin back in the ribbon and place a pin 3cm (1 1/8") down the ribbon and two more pins 1.5cm (5/8") apart. Push the anchor pin into the top of the ball and lay the ribbon alongside the newly created sixteenth lines and mark where the pins cross the line (*Fig.2*). Repeat on each on the sixteenth segment lines.

f) Use a third coloured pen to join up the dots to create the first zigzag line. Start on an eighth line (drawn first) at the first dot 4.5cm down from the top. Draw a line up towards the first 3cm mark on the sixteenth line to the right. Then draw a line downwards to the 4.5cm mark. Continue around the ball creating the first zigzag line.

g) To create the second zigzag line start at the second dot, 6cm down the first eighth segment line and draw upwards to the second dot, 4.5cm down the sixteenth segment line, and then down the 6cm dot on the next eighth segment line. Continue around the ball.

h) Make the third zigzag line in a similar way. You now have three zigzag lines giving you two bands around the ball.

4. **For the 10cm and 12cm balls:** These are made with the same measurements but the larger 12cm ball has an extra band.

a) Place an anchor pin near one end of a piece of ribbon and another pin 6cm (2 3/8") down from the top.

For the 10cm ball place *three* more pins at 2cm ($^3/_4$") intervals.

For the 12cm ball place *four* more pins at 2cm ($^3/_4$") intervals.

b) Push the first anchor pin into the top of the ball and lay the ribbon along a vertical eighth segment line. Make marks where the pins cross the line, and repeat for each eighth segment line (*Fig.1*).

c) Remove the marker pins from the ribbon.

d) Use the ribbon to divide the eighths in half, using a different colour pen. You now have sixteen vertical segment lines. These latest lines are referred to as the 'sixteenth' lines.

e) Put the first anchor pin back in the ribbon and place a pin 3cm ($1^1/_8$") down the ribbon. For the 10cm ball place *three* more pins at 2cm ($^3/_4$") intervals.
For the 12cm ball place *four* more pins at 2cm ($^3/_4$") intervals.

f) Push the anchor pin into the top of the ball and lay the ribbon alongside the newly created sixteenth lines. Mark where the pins cross the line and repeat for each sixteenth segment line (*Fig.2*).

g) Use a third coloured pen to join up the dots to create the zigzag line. Start on an eighth segment line (drawn first) at the first dot, 6cm down. Draw a line upwards towards the first dot, 3cm down on the sixteenth segment line to the right. Then go down towards the 6cm dot on the next eighth segment line. Continue around the ball.

h) To create the second zigzag line start at the second dot, 8cm down, on the first eighth segment line and draw upwards to the

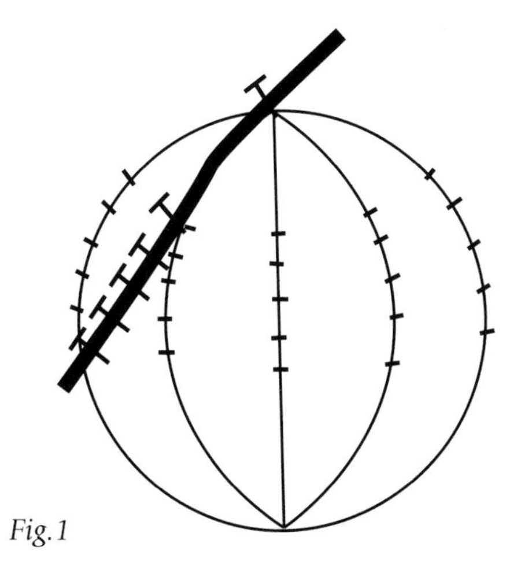

Fig.1

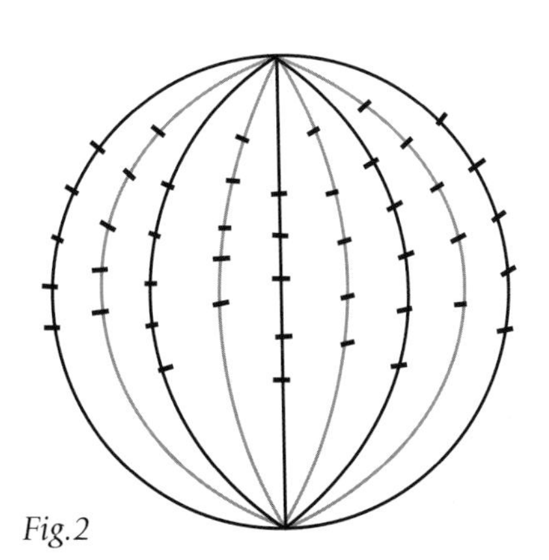

Fig.2

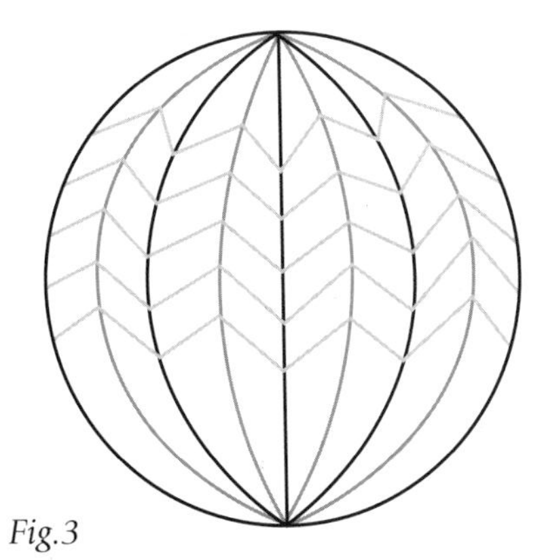

Fig.3

second dot on the sixteenth segment line and back down. Continue around the ball. Make the remaining zigzag lines in the same way.

5. For all balls cut the zigzag lines marked with the third coloured pen. Cut the lines of the first eighth vertical segment lines all the way down the ball (*Fig.3*).

6. Insert the hanging loop (see Design 1, steps 4–6, pages 14 and 15).

7. The fabrics are going to be small pieces in an inverted V shape. To estimate the size, lay a thin piece of paper over the largest central zigzag band and roughly trace off the shape. Allow a 1cm (3/8") margin of fabric when cutting out. You can either work all around one band horizontally in the same fabric or you can work down the ball using different colours. This way you can try out different colour combinations. If, when you have put all the fabrics in place you don't like any of them, it is easy to remove and replace them. So, audition your colour combinations. Once the bands are in place put in the top sections and then the bottom diamonds using the fabric templates provided.

8. For the beading use 3mm beading and do the zigzag lines first. Then put in the eighth segment lines.

9. Finish the ball in the usual way. Refer to Design 1, steps 11–12, page 16.

Design No. 13 – The Balloon Ball

Ball	**7cm Ball**	**10cm Ball**	**12cm Ball**
Fabric	30cm (12")sq of 3 diff fabrics	30cm (12")sq of 5 diff fabrics	30cm (12")sq of 6 diff fabrics
3mm gold ribbon	50cm (20")	60cm (3/4yd)	1m (1yd)
3mm beaded trim	2m (2yds)	3.75m (4yds)	4.25m (4 2/3yds)
Top finding + beads and corsage or hat pins. Short pins			

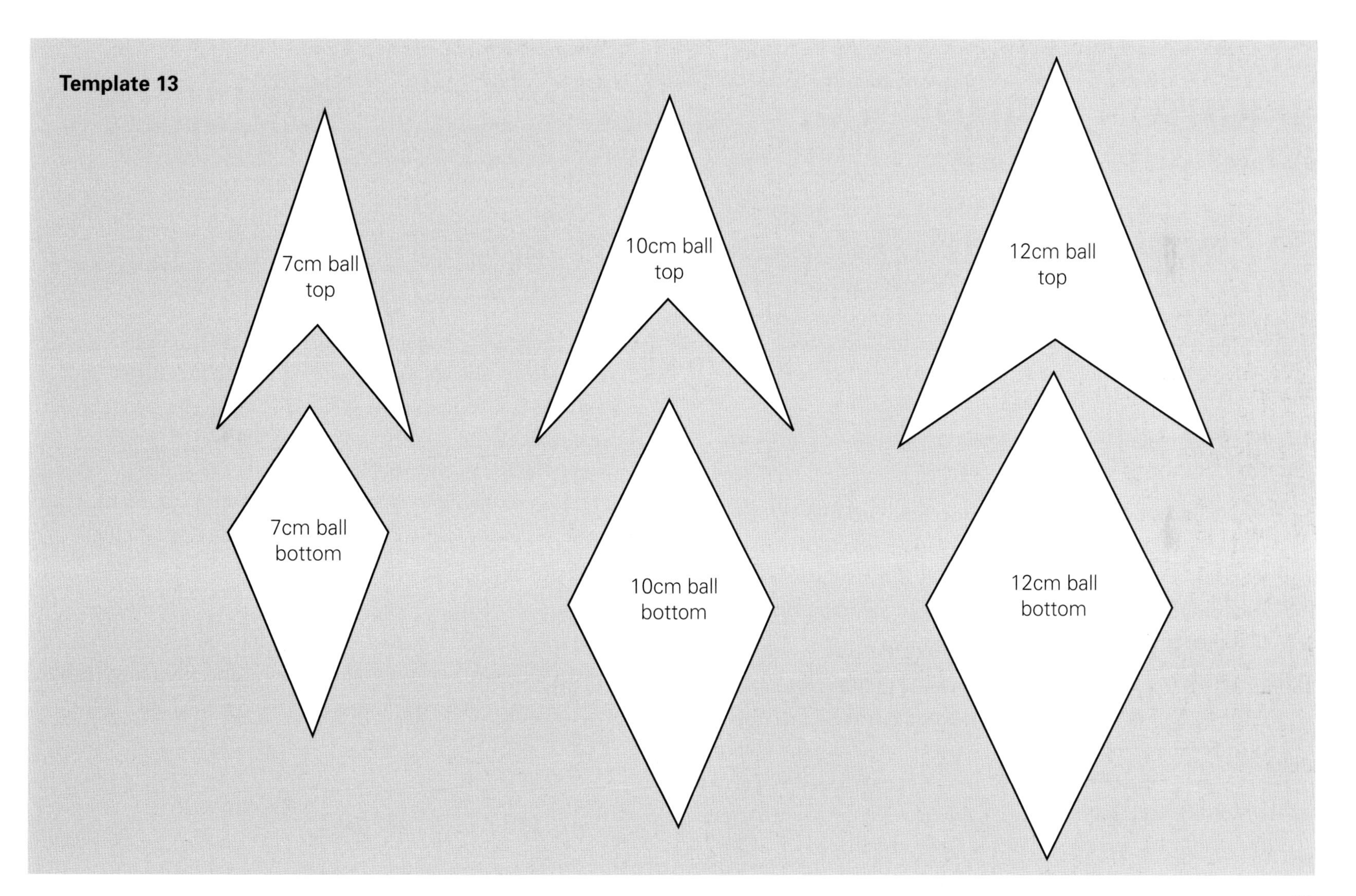
Template 13
7cm ball top
10cm ball top
12cm ball top
7cm ball bottom
10cm ball bottom
12cm ball bottom

DESIGN NO. 14
BRIGHTON PAVILION

Refer to the colour photograph page 60

The instructions given here are for a 12cm ball only. It can be done on a 10cm ball but is too complicated for a 7cm ball.

This design was inspired by the domes of Brighton Pavilion built in the early part of the 19th century on Britain's south coast. I have worked on a 12cm ball, using sequined and microdot foil fabrics.

1. Mark the top and bottom.
2. Divide the ball into eight segments (see Design 1, step 2, page 14).
3. Where the vertical segment line crosses the circumference draw a circle with a 3.5cm ($1\frac{1}{2}$") diameter, using a piece of ribbon as described in Design 10, step 2, page 52. Alternatively you could trace around the template on page 73 and pin it in place. Draw the circle in a second coloured pen.
4. Using a thin piece of ribbon as a measure put the anchor pin near one end of the ribbon. Put a second pin 3cm ($1\frac{1}{4}$") along the ribbon and a third pin 6cm ($2\frac{1}{2}$") along. Push the anchor pin into the top of the ball and make a mark where the 3cm pin crosses the segment line, and a mark between the segments, in the middle, at the 6cm point (*Fig.1*). Repeat the process at the bottom of the ball.
5. Join up the dots to form a zigzag line around the top and bottom of the ball (*Fig.2*). Mark in the segment lines above and below the circles in the second colour as shown by the light line in *Fig.2*.
6. Cut along the segment lines drawn with the second colour, make the hanging loop and insert the fabrics following Design 1, Steps 3–6, pages 14 and 15.
7. Start the beading by putting in the zigzag line around the top and bottom. Then place the beading around the circles. The vertical segment lines begin and end at the circles. Push the start of the beading well down into the crack under the beading round the circles and run it up, across the top of the ball, ending at the top of the circle directly opposite. When the top has been done in this way, up-end the ball and do the same for the bottom half.
8. To finish the ball add a finding and corsage pin to the top following Design 1, steps 11–12, page 16. At the bottom I have used a long pin with beads and a cone shaped finding. I have also pinned a little sequin flower in the centre of alternative circles. Experiment!

Fig.1

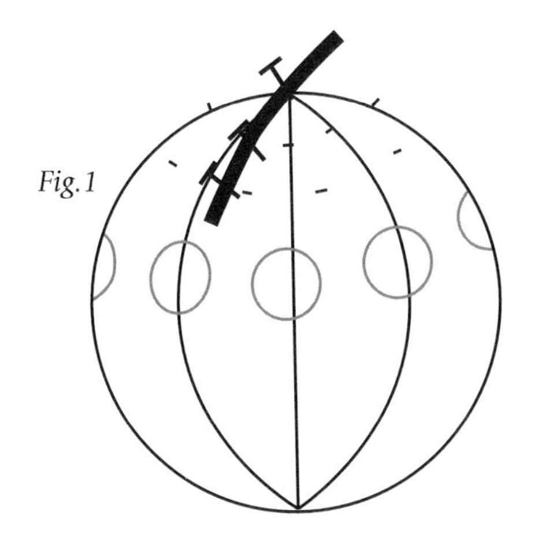

Fig.2

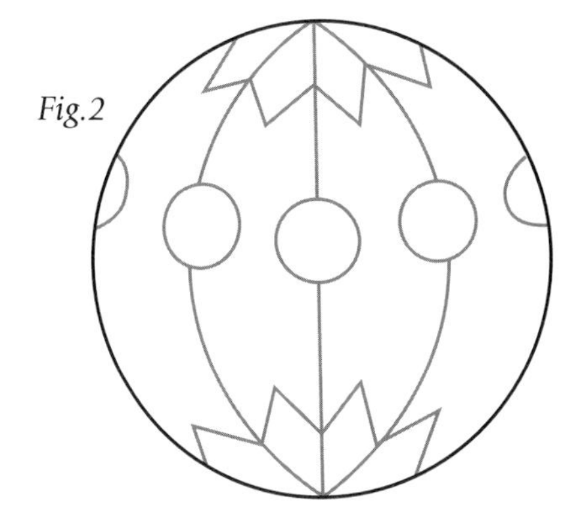

Design No. 14 – Brighton Pavilion

Ball	**12cm ball**
Fabric – for circles	25 x 25cm (10" x 10")
Fabric – top diamond	20 x 20cm (8" x 8")
Fabric – main section	30 x 35cm (12" x 14")
Fabric – bottom diamond	20 x 20cm (8" x 8")
3mm gold ribbon	1m (1yd)
3mm beaded trim	3.5m (4yds)

Top finding + corsage pin. Large pin + beads and finding for bottom. Short pins

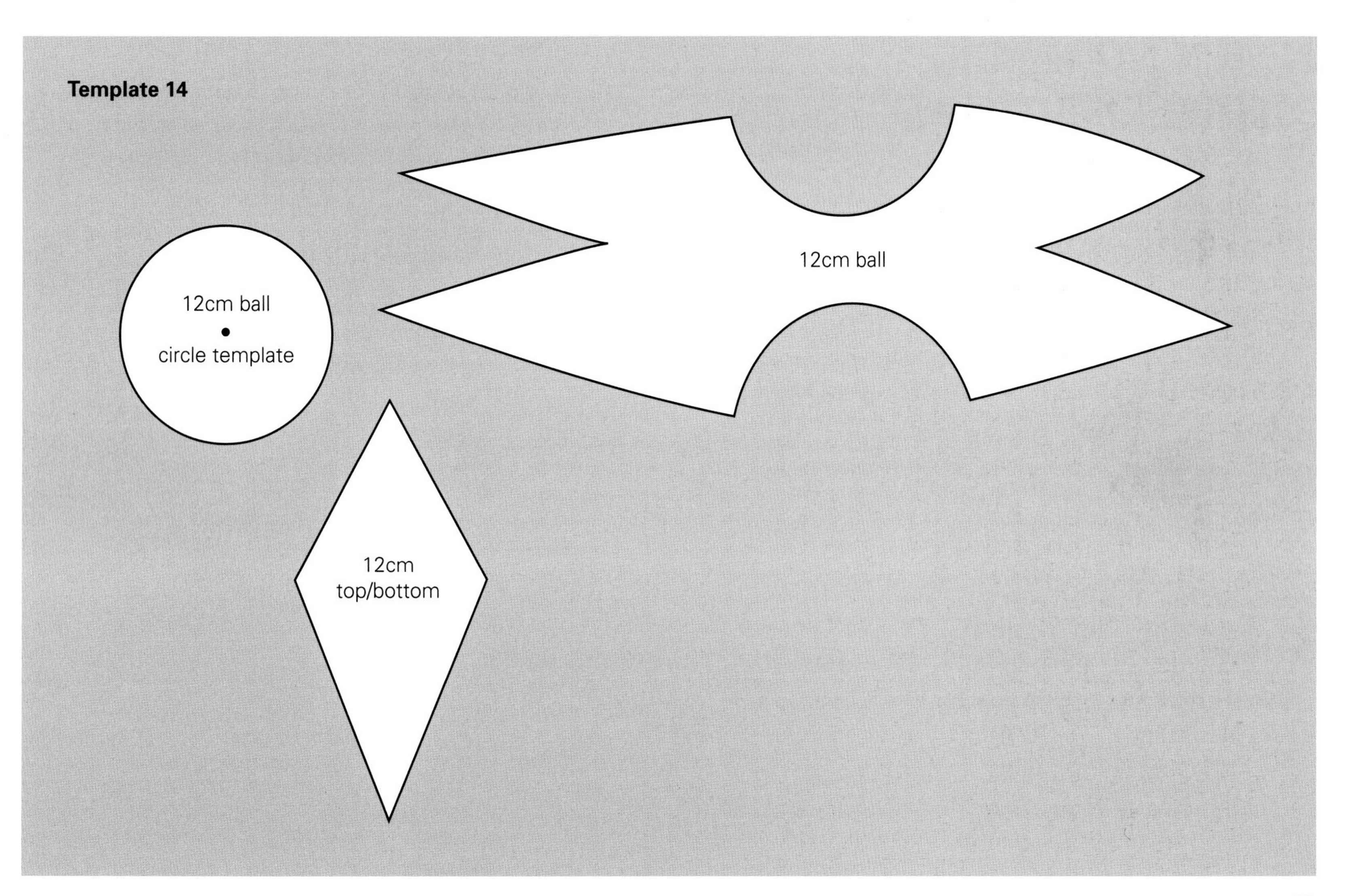
Template 14
12cm ball
12cm ball
circle template
12cm
top/bottom

DESIGN NO 15
FOLDED RIBBON BALL

Refer to the colour photograph page 64

The instructions given here are for a 7cm ball only, however the same technique may easily be applied to any sized ball.

This bauble is covered with plain gold fabric before being decorated with folded ribbon and some gold beads. On a bigger ball I would add extra rows of folded ribbon.

1. Mark the top and bottom of the ball and divide the ball into sixths following Design 4, step 1, page 24.
2. Cut the ball and insert the hanging loop (Design 1, steps 3–5, pages 14 and 15).
3. Next cover the ball with the fabric. The template for a segment one sixth of a 7cm ball is given in Design 4, page 25.
4. Pin the beading in place over the six segment lines.
5. Cut 12 rectangles of ribbon double the ribbon width. Fold the top two corners down to the middle to form a triangle. See Design 11, *Figs.4 and 5*, page 55.
6. Pin a row of ribbon triangles around the middle of the ball, lining up the point of the triangle with the line of beading. Turn the ball *upside down* and pin another row of triangles around the middle, see *Figs.1 and 2*.
7. Measure a piece of ribbon a bit longer than the circumference of the ball. Fold the long edges in so that they overlap and then using a bead on a pin place a row of beaded pins along the middle of the ribbon to keep it in place.
8. Finish in the usual way by adding a finding top and bottom with a hat or corsage pin, follow Design 1, steps 11–12, page 16.

Design No. 15 – Folded Ribbon Ball

Ball	**7cm ball**
Fabric	33 x 14cm (13" x 5 1/2")
3mm gold ribbon	50 (20")
3mm beaded trim	75cm (1yd)
25mm (1") Ribbon	1m (1yd)
Small gold beads	12

Top finding + bottom finding + hat or corsage pin. Short pins.

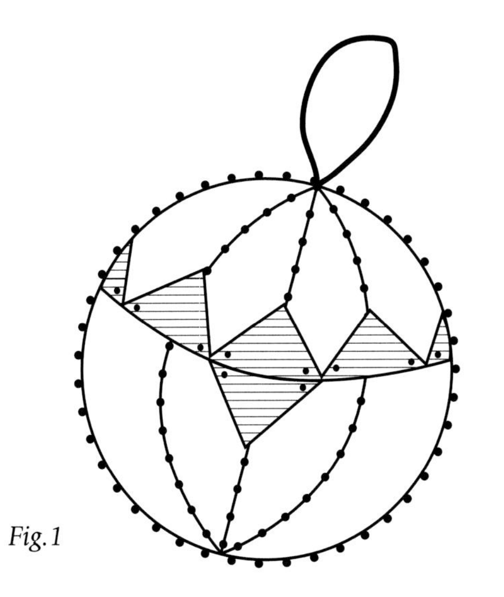

Fig.1

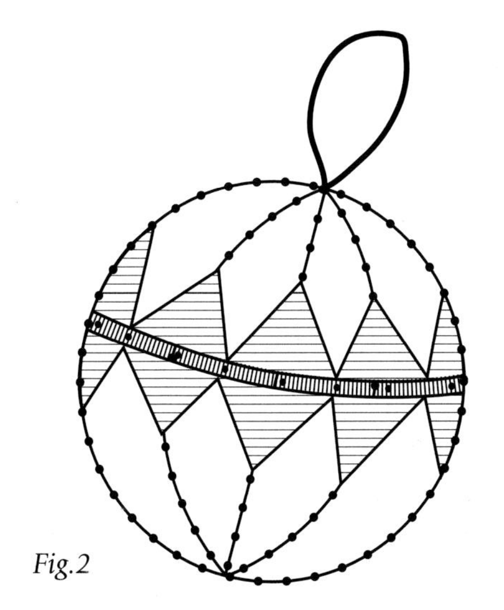

Fig.2

DESIGN NO. 16
PLEATED RIBBON BALL

Refer to the colour photograph page 64

The instructions given here are for a 7cm ball only. The same technique may easily be applied to any sized ball but you would need to use a wider ribbon on a larger ball.

There are various ways of pleating and manipulating ribbon. This is one of my favourites. You can use it to decorate baskets or even the Christmas cake!

1. Mark the top and bottom of the ball. Divide a 7cm ball into sixths (see Design 4, step 1, page 24).

2. Cut the lines, insert the hanging loop and put the fabrics in place following Design 1, steps 3–5, pages 14 and 15 and using the fabric template for Design 4, page 25. I have not used beading here but you could if you wish put it down the vertical lines now following Design 1, step 10, page 16.

3. To make the pleated ribbon you will need about three times the desired finished length so one metre (1yd) will be sufficient. If the ribbon is wired the pleats will be even easier to make.

4. To create the basic pleat fold the ribbon as shown (*Fig.1*) and secure with pins. To help me be accurate I cut a piece of card 1cm (1/2") wide to use as a measure. Place the piece of card on the ribbon at the left hand end and fold the ribbon back over it. Remove the piece of card and place it behind the ribbon abutting the fold. Fold the ribbon around the card, abutting the folds at the back. When you have pinned a few pleats backstitch through all the layers down the middle. Next thread a needle and bring it up in the middle of the pleat. Pull the edges of the pleat towards each other (*Fig.2*) and secure with a few stitches. Sew a little gold bead on. Do the same for each pleat.

5. When you have sufficient pleats to go around the ball, pin the ribbon in place around the middle of the ball with a small pin topped with a gold bead along the top and bottom ribbon edges.

6. Finish as usual. See Design 1, steps 11–12, page 16.

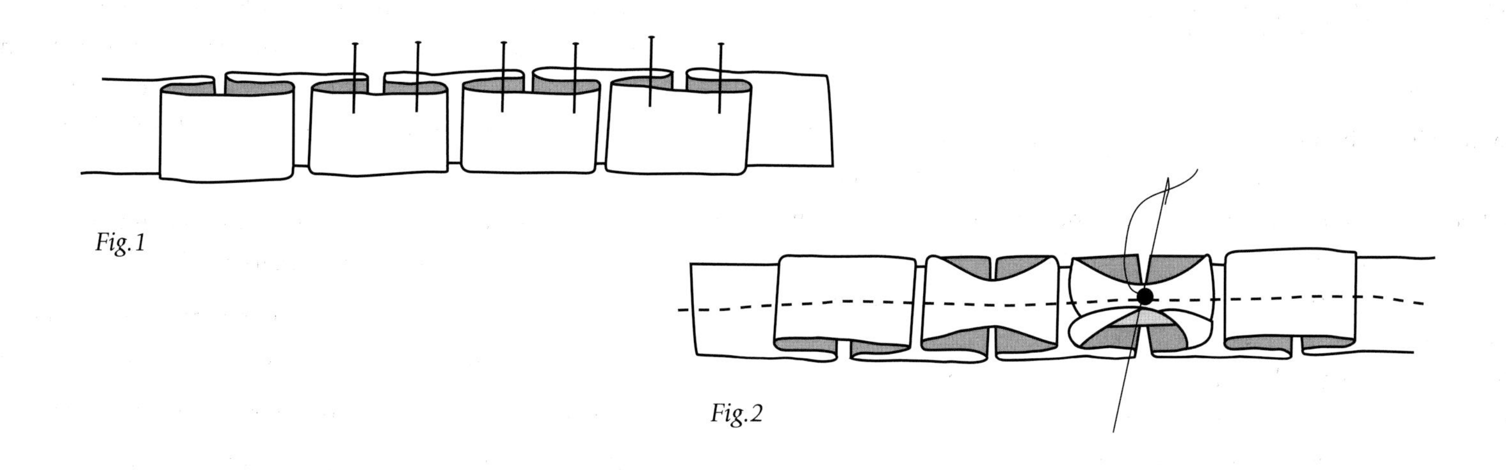
Fig. 1

Fig. 2

Design No. 16 – Pleated Ribbon Ball

Ball	**7cm ball**
Fabric	33 x 14cm (13" x 5 1/2")
3mm gold ribbon	50cm (20")
3mm beaded trim, if desired	75cm (30")
25mm (1") ribbon	1m (1yd)
Small gold beads + short pins	30
Top finding + bottom finding or bead and corsage pin	

RIBBON WEAVING

Introduction

Weaving with ribbon has been around a long time. The word 'wife' is derived from the verb to weave. Ribbons as we think of them today have been with us since the 16th century, becoming really popular in the following century. I have a charming little book published in 1895 by a school mistress describing how to teach weaving in paper, string, ribbon, straw and cane. So if you have never done any ribbon weaving do have a go. The hearts can be made in an evening and the wonderful sheen of the satin ribbons shows up beautifully on the tree. You can stuff the hearts with dried lavender (using a small funnel) and hang them in your wardrobe for the rest of the year if you wish. I have used just two colours so that you can see how different the patterns look. There are endless possibilities.

General Materials Needed for all Woven Hearts

The following is an outline of the materials required to make the hearts. Check that you have these before sorting out the specific requirements which are given with each design.

1. A cork tile, cork notice board or square of thick cardboard to use as a base. Not only do you need to stick pins in this base but you will need to put a hot iron on it.
2. Iron-on interfacing – This is placed on top of the cork base. The ultra soft or a really lightweight one is the best as it enables you to turn the heart inside out more easily. The interfacing has a layer of adhesive on it and the ribbons are going to be bonded on to it creating a piece of material. The technique is the same whatever the size. I made a waistcoat entirely of ribbons including the back.
3. A square of backing material for the heart – plain or patterned cotton or silk or anything you have to hand.
4. Thread – Invisible thread for sewing the cord in place and some ordinary sewing thread to match the ribbons and backing fabric.
5. Pins are needed to secure the ribbons to the cork board
6. Needle preferably with a blunt end and large eye, or a bodkin for doing the actual weaving
7. Ribbons – a detailed list of requirements is given with each design. There are an amazing variety of ribbons available today. As these are small hearts I used narrow ribbons made of polyester satin. You can use single face or double face. The gold and silver lamé ribbon comes in 6mm and 3mm widths.
8. Small quantity of thin ribbon is needed to make a hanging loop and a bow,
9. Flower or some sort of trim for a finishing decoration.

10. Cord – I like to edge all my hearts with gold or silver cord. This neatens the appearance of the heart and frames it adding extra sparkle. I put the cord in place and just over-sew it with invisible thread.
11. Lastly you need some stuffing material.
12. Read the full instructions given with Design 17 before completing the other woven designs.

DESIGN NO. 17
PLAIN WEAVE RIBBON HEART

Refer to the colour photograph page 83

This is the simplest form of weaving and is most effective.

1. The piece of interfacing has a textured side, this is the side with the adhesive on it. The interfacing needs to be pinned to the cork tile or board *glue side uppermost*. This is very important.

2. Pin pieces of the 7mm burgundy ribbon from top to bottom across the piece of interfacing (*Fig.1*). These are the warp ribbons. The ribbons should lie next to each other snugly but not overlapping. You should not be able to see any of the white interfacing showing, but you only need to go just beyond it.

3. Thread the large-eyed blunt-ended needle or bodkin with the 6mm gold ribbon and weave it over and under the burgundy ribbon, pinning the ribbon at each end (*Fig.2*). Continue like this, making sure you keep the ribbons straight and pushed close together. They have a habit of dipping in the middle.

4. When the interfacing square has been completely covered by ribbons, remove the pins very carefully from one corner. Place a piece of clean paper over the ribbons to protect them and press with a hot dry iron. Continue to remove pins and press. This will bond the ribbons to the interfacing. Check to see that this has happened. If it has not, either you did not have the interfacing the glue side uppermost or the iron is not hot enough to create the bond. When the ribbons have bonded turn the ribbon fabric over and press firmly on the back.

5. Place the heart template in the middle of the back and draw the heart outline making sure the line is clearly visible and the heart is centred in the middle of the square.

6. Either backstitch by hand or use the sewing machine to make a line of stitching outside the heart outline. This helps stabilise the ribbons.

7. Place the backing fabric on to the ribbon fabric, right sides together. Stitch around the heart outline leaving a gap at the top. Turn inside out and carefully push out the point.

8. Stuff the heart.

9. Push one end of the cord into the gap and using invisible thread oversew the cord all the way around the heart over the seam. Push the remaining end into the gap, turning in the raw edges of the fabric and ribbon fabric.

10. Before you close the gap, fold the piece of 3mm gold ribbon in half to form a loop and push both ends firmly down into the heart and close the gap, stitching through the ribbon loop to secure it.

11. Finally stitch your chosen trim in place. I attached a little rose and ribbon trim as a final decoration.

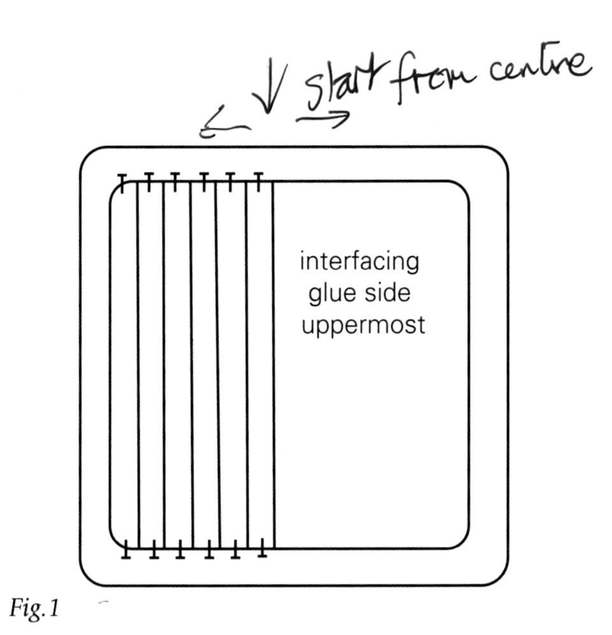

Fig.1

Fig.2

Design No. 17 – Plain Weave Ribbon Heart

Ultra soft iron-on interfacing	15.5cm (6")square
Backing fabric + matching thread	15.5cm (6")square
3mm gold lamé ribbon for hanging loop	25cm (12")
Decorative trim	Gold or burgundy
4mm gold cord + invisible thread	45cm (1/2yd)
7mm burgundy satin ribbon	4m (4 1/3yds)
6mm gold lamé ribbon	4m (4 1/3yds)

Weaving requirements

Design Nos. 17, 18 and 19 –
Plain Weave Ribbon Heart, Ribbed
Heart, and Zig-zag Weave Ribbon Heart

DESIGN NO. 18
RIBBED HEART

Refer to the colour photograph page 83

This design uses more ribbon but gives a textured look to the plain weave.

1. Pin the piece of interfacing to the board *glue side uppermost*. Lay the warp pieces of ribbon in the following order:
   7mm burgundy, 3mm gold, 3mm burgundy, 3mm gold ending with either a 7mm burgundy or 3mm burgundy ribbon.
   Repeat until the interfacing is covered (*Fig.1*).

2. Weave the weft ribbons in the following order:
   Row 1 – 7mm burgundy – over 1, under 1
   Row 2 – 3mm gold – under 1, over 1
   Row 3 – 3mm burgundy – over 1, under 1
   Row 4 – 3mm gold – under 1, over 1
   Repeat (*Fig.2*)

8. Complete the heart following Design 17, steps 4–11, page 80.

For additional information on making this design refer to the instructions given with Design 17, page 80.

Fig.1

Fig.2

Design No. 18 – Ribbed Heart

Ultra soft iron-on interfacing	15.5cm (6") square
Backing fabric + matching thread	15.5cm (6") square
Decorative trim	Gold or burgundy
4mm gold cord + invisible thread	45cm (1/2yd)
3mm gold ribbon (including hanging loop)	6m (6 1/2yds)
7mm burgundy ribbon	3.25m (3 1/2yds)
3mm burgundy ribbon	2.75m (3yds)

Ring of Hearts requirements

Design No. 20 – Ring of Hearts

Template 17

leave open

ribbon weaving heart

Template 20

DESIGN NO. 19
ZIGZAG WEAVE HEART

Refer to the colour photograph page 83

This creates another striking design.

1. Pin the piece of interfacing to the board *glue side uppermost.* Lay the warp pieces of ribbon in the following order, start with the burgundy then lay alternating gold and burgundy, ending with burgundy.

2. Weave the weft ribbons as follows:
   Row 1 – gold – over 2, under 2, over 2 under 2. Repeat until end.
   Row 2 – burgundy – under 1, then repeat over 2, under 2, over 2, until the end
   Row 3 – gold – under 2, over 2, under 2, over 2. Repeat until end.
   Row 4 – burgundy – over 1, then repeat under 2, over 2, under 2 until end.
   Repeat this sequence of 4 rows as necessary.

9. Complete the heart following Design 17, steps 4–11, page 80.

For additional information on making this design refer to the instructions given with Design 17, page 80.

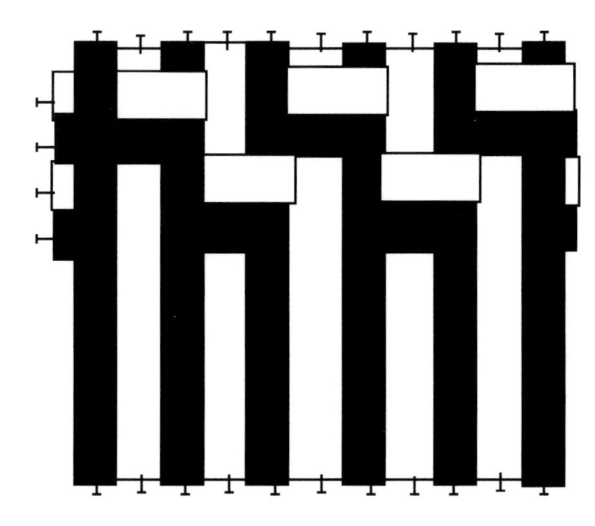

Fig. 1

Design No. 19 – Zigzag Weave Heart

Ultra soft iron-on interfacing	15.5cm (6") square
Backing fabric + matching thread	15.5cm (6") square
3mm gold lamé ribbon for hanging loop	25cm (12")
Decorative trim	Gold or burgundy
4mm gold cord + invisible thread	45cm (1/2yd)
6mm gold lamé ribbon	4.25m (4 1/2yds)
7mm burgundy ribbon	4.25m (4 1/2yds)

DESIGN NO. 20
RING OF HEARTS

Refer to the colour photograph page 87

Template on page 89

Continuing with the theme of hearts I combined twelve to make a 'Ring of Hearts'. You can use any colour scheme – creams and lilacs or pinks for a bedroom, perhaps checks and stripes for a more homespun look or Christmas fabrics as I have used here. The hearts are slightly smaller than the ribbon weaving hearts.

This is an opportunity to empty out your scrap basket and bits and pieces box, use up odd beads, sequins and buttons. You can make the hearts as simple or as embellished as you wish (or time permits). I usually let the pattern of the fabric dictate the decoration. If there are holly berries I put on gold or red beads; if stars, tiny sequin stars and so on. These all add texture, interest and reflect the light beautifully. The possibilities for experimentation are enormous.

You will need:

- 12 different 13cm (5") squares of fabric
- 12 x 13cm (5") squares of backing fabric
- 5m of 4mm gold cord ($5^1/_4$yds)
- 12 trimmings
- assortment of round beads, bugles, sequins
- invisible thread
- stuffing
- matching threads
- 26cm (10") metal florist's ring used for making Christmas wreaths

1. Draw around the template given (*Template 20*, page 89) on the back of a piece of patterned material. This is the stitching line so make sure you can see it.

2. Place this fabric on top of the backing fabric, right sides together and backstitch or machine around the heart outline from A to B leaving the gap open. For one of the hearts in the photo I have layered up a piece of gold net on top of a plain gold coloured cotton fabric.

3. Turn inside out and stuff.

4. As for the ribbon weaving hearts, insert one end of a piece of cord into the gap and using invisible thread oversew the cord in place all the way around, pushing the other end into the gap. Close up the gap.

5. Sew on any decorations you think will enhance your heart and sew a trimming where the two pieces of cord meet. I find it easier to sew on all the embellishments after I have made and stuffed the heart. There are several reasons. If you put the

embellishments on before joining the fabric to the backing it is difficult for either the machine or your needle to avoid all the beads etc. If I put the embellishments on before stuffing I often manage to sew the backing to the front inadvertently. It is also much easier to lose your knots and ends of threads in the stuffing.

6. Arrange the hearts in a circle on the wire ring and either sew or pin in place. As long as you have enough hearts they do not seem to move around on the wire.

SUPPLIERS

Mail Order

Creative Beadcraft Ltd

Unit 2, Asheridge Business Centre

Asheridge Road, Chesham

Bucks HP5 2PT

Tel: 01494 778818

Fax: 01494 776605

Email: beads@creativebeadcraft.co.uk

Website: www.creativebeadcraft.co.uk

Denholme Velvets Ltd Mill Shop

Halifax Road

Bradford BD13 4EZ

Tel: 01274 839108

Mon – Fri 1pm – 5pm

Sat 9.30am – 4.30pm

Pinflair

Unit 9, Wareham's Lane

Hertford SG14 1LA

Tel: 01992 582712

Fax: 01992 505439

Email: pinflair@ntlworld.com

Website: www.pinflair.co.uk

Springwood House Designs

29 Nichols Way

Wetherby, West Yorks LS22 6AD

Tel/Fax: 01937 581276

The Viking Loom Ltd

22 High Petergate

York YO1 7EH

Tel/Fax: 01904 620587

Website: www.vikingloom.co.uk

Shops

Bombay Stores

Shearbridge Road

Bradford BD7 1NX

Tel: 01274 729993/729137

Fax: 01274 308515

Open 7 days 10am – 8pm

Creative Beadcraft Ltd

Ells & Farrier

20 Beak Street

London W1F 9RE

Tel: 020 7629 9964

Mon – Fri 9am – 5.15pm

Sat 10am – 5.15pm

Denholme Velvets Mill Shop

Halifax Road

Denholme

Bradford BD13 4EZ

Tel: 01274 839108

Mon – Fri 11am - 5pm

Sat 9.30am – 4.30pm

The Viking Loom

22 High Petergate

York YO1 7EH

Tel/Fax 01904 620587

Mon – Sat 9.30am – 5pm